CANYON VILLAGE
in
YELLOWSTONE

CANYON VILLAGE *in* YELLOWSTONE

THE MODEL FOR MISSION 66

LESLEY M. GILMORE

THE History PRESS

Published by The History Press
Charleston, SC
www.historypress.net

Front cover images, clockwise from top left: 1955 WB&A rendering of Canyon Village cabins. *Courtesy of AECOM*; groundbreaking ceremony for Canyon Village Lodge, June 25, 1956. *Photo by Haynes Studios Inc., courtesy of MHS RCPA Haynes Foundation Collection*; Canyon Village Visitor Center, 1958. *Photo by Haynes Studios Inc., courtesy of MHS RCPA Haynes Foundation Collection. Rear cover images, top to bottom*: 1955 WB&A interior rendering of Canyon Village Lodge. *Courtesy of AECOM*; 1961 Mission 66 brochure. *Courtesy of NPS, YNP, Coll. 185385 YELL 185385-67.*

First published 2017

Manufactured in the United States

ISBN 9781467119559

Library of Congress Control Number: 2016947534

CONTENTS

Acknowledgements 7
Introduction 11

1. Historical Background 13
2. Mission 66: The Federal Program 19
3. Mission 66: Disseminated by Memoranda 27
4. The Design History of Canyon Village 49
5. Mission 66 Modernist Design Features 79
6. Canyon Village Construction 91
7. Acceptance of Canyon Village 107
8. The Future of Mission 66 117

Notes 119
Bibliography 133
Index 137
About the Author 141

ACKNOWLEDGEMENTS

The paramount pleasure in preparing a book about a seminal Mission 66 design project in Yellowstone National Park comes from the many research connections that reinforce each other, propagating information, impressions, insights and valuable resources that help the story become more complete. Researching more recently constructed buildings has its advantages, providing the ability to learn from people who had direct contact with the design and/or the construction. The origins of this project stem from my working relationship with Mary Murphy, concessions specialist for Yellowstone National Park, until her retirement in December 2015. She engaged CTA Architects Engineers to prepare a Historic Structure Report for Canyon Village Lodge and its companion Administration Building, thus solidifying my interest in Mission 66 in the national parks. I remain grateful for the opportunity to explore this genre, and through the continuation of the project into a renovation of Canyon Village Lodge, Xanterra Parks & Resorts has reinforced its commitment to the preservation of Mission 66 as a concept. CTA provided me with research assistants Anna Claire Davis and Chelsea Holling and, more importantly, helped me dedicate the time necessary to complete this writing project. CTA president Scott Wilson's personal encouragement reflected the board of directors' support, for which I am grateful.

Early on in this process, I discovered that Bozeman architect George Mattson was the son of Yellowstone's landscape architect, Frank Mattson, who was a main character in Canyon Village's design. George also worked for McNeil Construction (MCC) at the site for two summers. He graciously shared information about the construction and his father. Yellowstone also has a web of people who will never break their ties with the Park and the people they've met doing (repeated) seasonal or full-time work at their wonderland. George Bornemann epitomizes this type, earning the moniker "Mr. Yellowstone" for his years working in the Park. His interest naturally led him to buy Park-related effects, including—most importantly—colored slides that the Haynes Photo Shop took of Canyon Village from the time of the groundbreakings to after the grand openings. George introduced to me to his friend Diane Papineau, whose master's thesis focused on the developments at Yellowstone's Grand Canyon from its formation to the present day. Her work, and sharing of images, helped direct my focus to the resource and man's response to it.

Yellowstone's resources run deep, with vast collections of photographs and archives, which I relied on heavily to piece together the sequence of events that led to construction of this inaugural Mission 66 project. I am most indebted to Colleen Curry, supervisory museum curator and Anne Foster, archivist, at the Yellowstone National Park Heritage and Research Center. Lory Morrow, curator of photography at the Montana Historical Society Research Center Photograph Archives (MHS RCPA) and guardian of the Haynes photo collection, enabled me to illustrate this publication with the colored images that George Bornemann loaned for this effort.

While the firm of Welton Becket & Associates (WB&A) is now under the umbrella of another firm (AECOM), the two sons, Welton Becket Jr. and Bruce Becket, as well as a nephew, MacDonald Becket, have given me the valuable bloodline links to Welton David Becket, the force behind the firm at the time Canyon Village was designed. They factor deeply in making me feel personally connected to its creation. AECOM is the current holder of the inspirational colored renderings created by Welton Becket & Associates as part of the Canyon Village design process. Without these images, the design intent of WB&A would be difficult to convey.

WB&A's archives are spread among several repositories: the Becket family members, UCLA Special Collections and the Getty Research Institute Special Collections. Early renditions of the construction documents for Canyon Village Lodge and the Recreation Hall provided a design chronology not previously understood. Yellowstone National Park's Herb Dawson, Peter Galindo and Sterling Smith dug deep to find construction documents for the cabins, Hamilton Store and Canyon

Village Lodge and Administration Building, respectively. Lisa Verwys at the Museum of the Rockies opened up the Hamilton Stores' collection of drawings for examination.

Penultimately, I must extend gratitude to Artie Crisp, who suggested this project to me and nudged me gently along the way. I would not have considered pursuing the additional research and writing for this book were it not for Artie.

Lastly, my loving husband, Bob Franzen, has stood by my often baffling process of researching and writing, infusing me with the energy needed to wrap it up.

INTRODUCTION

This is a Mission 66 project: Canyon Village.
—National Park Service

Canyon Village in Yellowstone National Park was the inaugural nationwide project for the National Park Service's initiative known as Mission 66. This federal program commenced in 1955 and was intended to be completed by 1966, at the fiftieth anniversary of the National Park Service (NPS, Park Service). The primary goal was to rectify the maintenance backlog from World War II funding diversions and the ever-increasing visitation to the national parks. Parallel goals were to accommodate greater numbers of automobiles in the national parks, to change the visitors' experience and to locate visitor facilities farther away from the natural features. This program was representative of other national trends—in conservation, architectural design and social improvement programs—and reflective of the optimism of the 1950s, as well as of the assurance that federal programs could help cure societal ills.

Conrad Wirth, the director of the National Park Service and the creator of Mission 66, selected Canyon Village of Yellowstone National Park—the first national park—as the inaugural project of the program. This new Canyon Village was located at a previously undeveloped site and included all the newly appointed necessary amenities easily accessed from a commodious horseshoe-shaped parking lot. NPS prepared the site and constructed the new visitor center. Private concessioners constructed the Canyon Lodge and Administration Building, Hamilton Store, Haynes Photo Shop, employee dormitories, Campers Services Building, the Service Station and five hundred visitor cabin rooms.

This large project was designed and constructed in an abbreviated period, subject to detailed NPS oversight and under pressure to be worthy of the inaugural (poster child) status. It was to be used as the example for the rest of the Mission 66 projects. Design, construction and programmatic use were scrutinized; the remaining projects would be fashioned after the positive aspects of this project and also benefit from alternative approaches resulting from lessons learned.

This book recounts how and why Canyon Village came to be the first Mission 66 project; what that meant in terms of coordination, design and construction both locally and nationally; how the completed project was received; and Canyon Village's current status. Mission 66 is currently criticized for not looking like the "Rustic Parkitecture" most have come to equate with the national park experience; this is part of a nationwide trend to dismiss the modern architecture of the 1950s and 1960s. Many, however, support the remaining Mission 66 projects as indicative of their time (i.e., having a valid place in history), and many of the younger generations find this architectural style stimulating. It is hoped that knowledge will generate and sustain understanding and support for Mission 66.

ABBREVIATIONS USED THROUGHOUT THE BOOK:

EODC = Eastern Office of Design & Construction
MCC = McNeil Construction Company
MHS = Montana Historical Society Research Center
MHS RCPA = Montana Historical Society Research Center Photograph Archives
NPS = National Park Service
NPS-YNP = Yellowstone National Park Archives, Heritage and Research Center
S&G = Stone & Glass Ltd.
WODC = Western Office of Design & Construction
YNP = Yellowstone National Park
YPC = Yellowstone Park Company

Chapter 1

HISTORICAL BACKGROUND

For the benefit and enjoyment of the people.
—The Act of Dedication

History of Yellowstone National Park

Yellowstone National Park was established as the first national park on March 1, 1872, with the provision "to protect, preserve and utilize the natural resources within its boundaries as a 'public park or pleasuring ground for the benefit and enjoyment of the people.' The Congress at that time recognized the great value and unusual character of the natural resources of Yellowstone."[1] Yellowstone National Park (YNP, Yellowstone or Park) is located in the northwest corner of Wyoming and extends over the borders into Montana to the north and Idaho to the west. Its 2.2 million acres were set aside to protect more than two hundred geysers, travertine terraces and other thermal features, as well as its abundant wildlife. The Park is just as well known for its magnificent bison, elk, coyotes, wolves, foxes, otters and bears (both grizzly and black). Heavily forested mountainous terrain and valleys provide cover and food for the wildlife; rushing rivers supply further sustenance. The Park history is interwoven with these natural features, which attracted and sustained the Native Americans and the errant fur traders who told crazed, unbelieved tales of the boiling sulfur springs, emerald pools, misty geysers and bubbling and burping muddy paint pots.

The conservation movement that embraced Yellowstone had been growing since creation of Yosemite as a state park in 1864. President Lincoln had signed the legislation for the State of California, setting the Yosemite Valley and Mariposa Big Tree Grove aside for preservation and public use. Yosemite National Park was established in 1890 in an effort to provide it with the greater protection of the federal government. These two parks form the backbone of many of the original philosophies and experiences of the National Park Service and have similar development histories.

The Congressional act did not provide the protection needed to fend off poachers of mineral deposits, timber and animals. The War Department took the reins from the Department of Interior in 1886, and in 1891 the U.S. Army constructed Fort Yellowstone in the Mammoth Hot Springs area near the north entry to the Park. Two years after it was created in 1916, the National Park Service (NPS or Park Service) received control of the Park.

To fulfill the mandate, the Park developed visitor accommodations based on carriage travel distances and feature locations. Hotels, tent camps and stores became increasingly larger and more elaborate to satisfy the typical visitor who could afford the train ride to the Park. Visits were often one to two weeks long. Concessioners were granted contracts to operate their businesses in the Park, provided they conducted business within the contractual parameters. The number of concessioners has reduced steadily over the years as the number of visitors has increased and the contractual stipulations grown more stringent. This has been concurrent with the increasingly sophisticated protection strategies for all the resources, including the reintroduction of a lost resource—the wolf—fire management, sustainability goals and even greater numbers of tourists.

The automobile was first introduced to Yellowstone in 1915 and has never been restricted. Tour buses also bring large groups into and through the Park. The main roadways are in a figure-eight configuration that accesses most of the features and all the sizable visitor services that provide overnight accommodations: Mammoth Hot Springs, Roosevelt, Grand Canyon of the Yellowstone, Yellowstone Lake, Grant Village and the Old Faithful geyser basins. Despite the seemingly endless amount of pavement dedicated to roads and parking lots, more than 95 percent of the Park is undeveloped. NPS director Newton Drury's statement in the 1948 *Haynes Guide* explains the Park Service's philosophy toward the parks:

> *Forests are protected for their beauty and interest and not as a source of lumber. The streams flow undammed. Millions of visitors each year use, but do not consume, the natural resources of the parks. Though it is necessary, for the enjoyment of visitors, to provide roads, campgrounds, overnight accommodations of various kinds, and other structures and utilities, the ideal is to keep these intrusions to a minimum and to design them so that they harmonize with the landscape. All but a small fraction of Yellowstone and other national parks remains as it was before the white man appeared on the American continent. Only in these parks is there assurance that Americans of the future will be able to see and enjoy some of the primitive wilderness of America as it was viewed by the trappers, the explorers and the pioneers.*[2]

The Park's visitation grew with the national population and decreased during World Wars I and II, as well as during the Great Depression in between. In the 1950s, the visitor services were in poor condition from neglect, as resources—funding and personnel—had been drawn toward the war effort. Visitation, however, was up, from fewer than 100,000 in 1944 to more than 1.3 million in 1954. Visitation was projected to increase 25 percent between 1960 and 1970.[3] The number of visitors has risen steadily to more than 4 million in 2015.

History of Tourist Accommodations at the Grand Canyon of the Yellowstone

The Grand Canyon of the Yellowstone River is the Park's second-most visited feature. It is a stunning rush of color and water amid 1,000-foot-deep canyons that thrill even the most indifferent visitor. The total drop is split into two falls: the Upper Falls, with a 109-foot drop, and the Lower Falls, with its 308-foot drop. In 1883, the Yellowstone Park Improvement Company constructed the first visitor accommodations close to the west rim of the Grand Canyon. This temporary tent hotel housed seventy-five guests and provided the comfort of spring mattresses and full dining services. No trace remains, yet it is known that the location was considered too close to the rim.[4] To prevent further location misjudgments, the Military Assistance Authorized for Protecting the Park—Sundry Civil Bill for 1883 was passed on March 3, 1883. This bill authorized the secretary of the interior to lease small land areas (less than ten acres) for periods not exceeding ten years, providing that the lease not include any geysers or "other objects of curiosity or interest in said park." Most specifically—and pertinent to the future developments at the Canyon—was the following clause restricting development on "any ground within one quarter of a mile of any of the geysers, or the Yellowstone Falls."[5] This quarter-mile distance would become known as the "sacred zone," which was later reduced to one-eighth of a mile. Ultimately, neither distance was deemed far enough.

In compliance with the 1883 act—and in an effort to not block the view of the falls—the more permanent hotels, erected in 1886 and 1891, were located farther from the rim of the falls. The latter hotel was well liked and comfortable yet deemed too small and ironically too far from the canyon and the falls. In addition, the soils were poor, causing the foundation to shift. The Yellowstone Park Transportation Company decided to build a new hotel in its stead. Harry Child, the mastermind behind the concession firm that would ultimately become the Yellowstone Park Company, engaged architect Robert Reamer to design the new Canyon Hotel, after the two toured great hotels in Europe: "The Grand Canyon Hotel would be built on the same site as the second hotel, despite Superintendent Pitcher's comments [that it was too far from the canyon] and despite known foundation problems from unstable soils. In fact, Reamer planned to incorporate the second hotel into his construction at its western end, modifying its roof to match."[6]

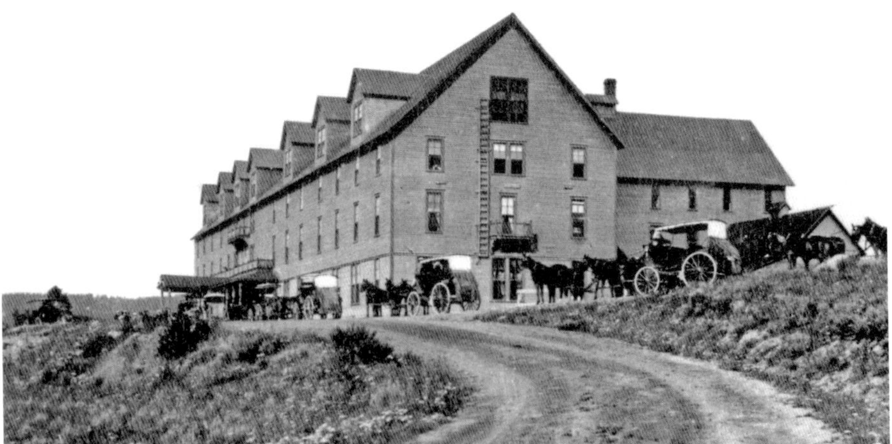

Second Canyon Hotel, after installation of dormers, circa 1901. *Courtesy NPS, YNP, YELL 14322-2.*

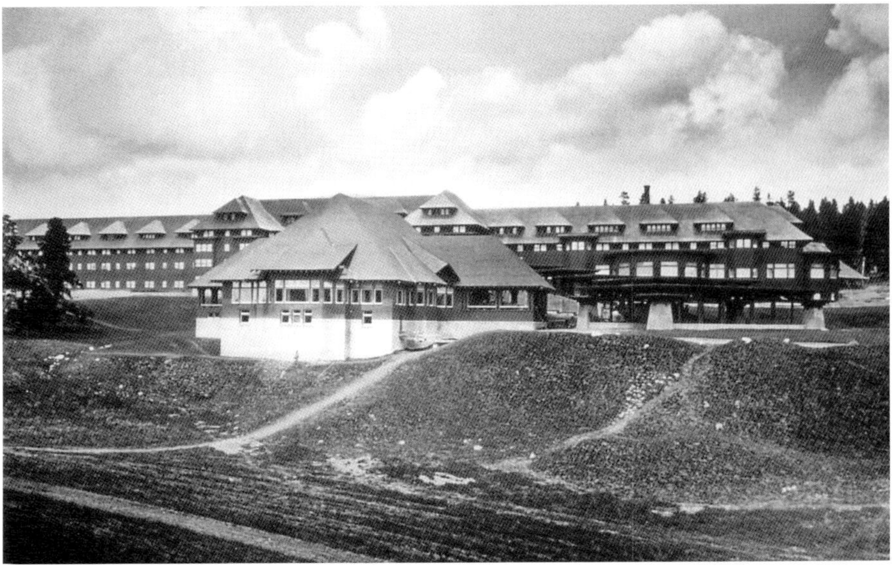

Third Canyon Hotel, designed by Robert Reamer and constructed 1909–11. The wing at the west (*left*) end of the image is the second hotel, with roofs modified to match the new construction.

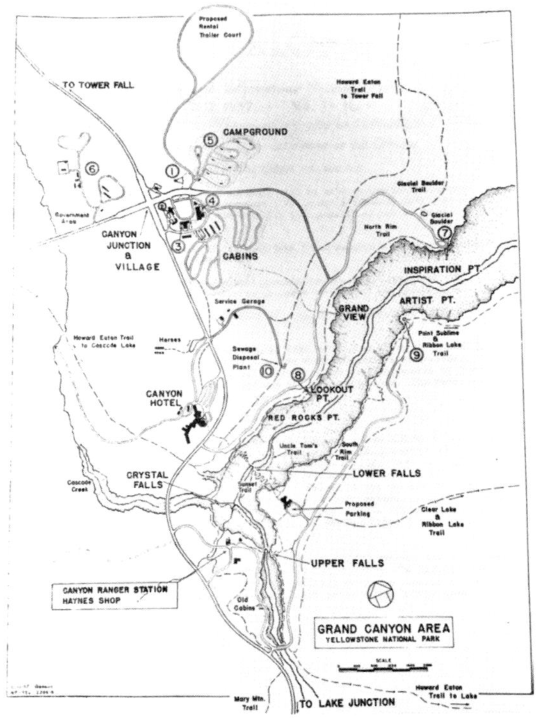

Grand Canyon Area: Yellowstone National Park, 1957, showing extant Canyon Hotel west of the Grand Canyon and the new Canyon Junction and Village to the north. *Courtesy NPS, YNP, YELL 185385-68.*

The new hotel, three stories with dormered attics, extended out from the earlier hotel (now a wing), reaching out toward the Lower Falls. This grand building quickly became and remained a favorite destination for numerous visitors. This hotel settled unevenly due to the hygroscopic soils, which factored into the ultimate decision to discontinue its use and demolish it after the new Canyon Village Lodge was completed in 1957. Canyon Hotel was the largest structure ever built in Yellowstone. In the 1920s, additional tourist accommodations were provided on either side of the Upper Falls, close to the rim, disregarding the quarter-mile setback. An auto camp, ranger station, Haynes Photo Shop and stores were on the west rim and the Canyon Lodge on the east. This pinch point spanning the Canyon was referred to as "Main Street."[7]

The Park began master planning in the 1930s, with the primary intent to relocate the functions away from the rim. These plans were deferred until the Mission 66 project of 1956.

Chapter 2

MISSION 66

THE FEDERAL PROGRAM

The people are loving the parks to death.
—*Conrad L. Wirth*

The Mission

Mission 66 was designed to make up for lost time—time lost primarily to World War II and the subsequent Cold War peacekeeping efforts. Work in the national parks—and at many other non-defense-related government agencies—had gained momentum during the Great Depression, greatly aided by the Civilian Conservation Corps and WPA/PWA programs. These energies and monetary infusions were subsequently diverted to the war efforts, which became the final exit strategy from the Depression. The Park Service's 1940 appropriation of nearly $35 million had plummeted in 1945 to less than $5 million. With World War II over, nationwide morale and traveling rose, unaccompanied by park improvements. "Loved to death"[8] became the mantra to describe the condition of the parks—heavily visited and run-down. This recipe for widespread disgruntlement was untenable. NPS director Conrad Wirth dreamed of—and implemented by will and collaboration—the remedy for this national disaster. While Conrad Wirth had strong and powerful supporters, it is doubtful that this plan would have come to life and thrived without him.

Conrad Wirth

Conrad Wirth had a vision. He was also at the right place and time, with his requisite long-term experience in the Park Service system and the fortitude of character to see it through. His used all his skills, training, experience and connections to create and implement Mission 66. In his 1980 book *Parks, Politics, and the People*, Wirth provides a clear trajectory of how this came to be and demonstrates that his was the tripartite collaboration to which the title alludes. His ample writings as director of the Park Service provide more detail and support the claims in his publication.

In 1899, Conrad was born into the world of landscape architecture and with the inherent drive to reserve and preserve parkland for the people. His father was a horticulturist and park planner who had been trained in Switzerland before immigrating to the United States in the late 1880s. He managed and developed parks in New York, Connecticut and Minnesota. Conrad continued in his father's shoes by studying landscape gardening at Massachusetts Agricultural College, a profession he defined as one "trained to provide plans for land uses that will best serve, over the long term, the environmental requirements of the people."[9] After graduating with a bachelor's degree in 1924, Wirth worked for a private landscape design firm in New Orleans, yet soon after, in 1928, he began his government career in Washington, D.C., with a position at the National Capital Park and Planning Commission. His experience and contacts there soon led him to a position with the National Park Service. He began at the Branch of Land Planning in 1931, working under Director Horace Albright. Wirth was fortunate for this connection to the 1916 origin of the Park Service; the direct lineage from NPS creator Steven Mather to the second NPS director Horace Albright gave Wirth keen insights into the purpose of the agency and the directorship that he would ultimately hold from 1951 until his retirement in 1964. Early in his service, he found himself surrounded by "Mather men."[10]

Conrad directed the Civilian Conservation Corps' program in the state parks from its inception in 1933 to its dissolution in 1942. In this capacity, he became familiar with parks across the United States, organizing large and complex manpower efforts, as well as the value of conservation efforts. This became a model for the Mission 66 program he would initiate as director of the Park Service. Wirth used his political and Park Service connections to create this program, inspiringly crowning his thirty-three-year career with the Park Service.

CARRYING OUT MASTER PLANS FROM THE 1920s AND 1930s

The whole purpose of Mission 66 was to update and carry out the National Park Service's master plans.[11]

In launching "MISSION 66" (as Wirth typically wrote it), Wirth was providing the parks with a means to implement master plans that had languished since the 1920s and 1930s. Wirth had been directly involved in some of these and thus understood the real needs of the parks. He perceived it as his mission to revive these plans, update them as required and see them through. In preparation for this grand scheme, Wirth reorganized the Park Service in 1951, appointing regional concession supervisors and park-specific concession chiefs, eliminating a layer of bureaucracy. He created two new branch offices to centralize control of design, composed of staff who had been located in the regional offices: the Western Office of Design & Construction (WODC) and an eastern one (EODC). In February 1955, he launched a Mission 66 Steering Committee, which later evolved into an Advisory Committee, both chaired by Lon Garrison (who would later be chosen to serve as Yellowstone National Park's superintendent for nearly the duration of Mission 66, from November 1956 to February 16, 1964), and a Mission 66 Committee (of Park Service staff). Wirth and the committees felt a sense of mission and urgency, determining that a ten-year plan, if well organized and well funded, would correct the poor condition of the park facilities, provide for vastly increased numbers of visitors, remove inappropriate resort-like development in the parks and respond to the increased number of private automobiles in the parks. This tall order was demanded by the public and critics, and implementation would be nearly complete by the Golden (Fiftieth) Anniversary of the National Park Service.

Wirth worked closely with his staff, the committees and the secretary of the interior to request and review ten-year prospectuses submitted by the parks. This gave them a list of projects (some nearly shovel-ready, having been in the works since the 1930s) and the funding requirements. The secretary of the interior lobbied President Eisenhower in February 1956, explaining the motivation and anticipated benefits of Mission 66:

> *A critical problem faces our National Parks.*
>
> *The desire of many Americans to spend their growing leisure in the great open spaces of the National Parks and in visiting our historic shrines has raised attendance from twenty-one million in 1946 to fifty million*

last year, with eighty million expected by 1966. The result has been an increasingly serious overcrowding of the park facilities: of accommodations, campgrounds, ranger services—everything...

Under this Administration substantial gains have been made toward meeting the needs of the visitors to our Park system. The dramatic increases in attendance, however, now call for accelerated action...

After thorough study, the Director of the National Park Service and I, have prepared an action program which faces this task squarely. It is called Mission 66—a proposed ten-year development plan which should begin now and should equip and staff the Park areas to serve the needs of the expected 80,000,000 visitors by 1966, the 50th anniversary year of the National Park Service.

Carrying forward Mission 66 will result in improved roads, more campgrounds and facilities for visitor use, and should stimulate investment of private capital in modern accommodations. At the same time, it will preserve the historic, the wilderness, and other features of the areas. It will satisfy the demand for more of such ranger services to the public as lectures, exhibits, and guided tours. It will strengthen the Government's partnership with the states, counties and cities in meeting total recreational requirements.

In short Mission 66 covers all the anticipated needs of the Parks, plots a comprehensive and well-balanced schedule of improvement, and starts immediately. It fulfils the pledge you made in the State of the Union Message.

I have the honor to transmit the Mission 66 program for your consideration. I strongly recommend your approval to start putting it into effect immediately as a vital part of this Administration's resources conservation program.[12]

This letter states it all: the ill effects of overcrowding, the need for accelerated action, the improvements required and the reminder that Eisenhower had pledged to help the parks. Eisenhower responded as anticipated, immediately sending a letter to the House Speaker and vice president. His February 2 letter was a concise summary of the secretary's letter and requested an amendment to the 1957 budget to address these needs without delay. The 1957 fiscal year budget for the Park Service was increased from $4.4 million to $12.5 million.

Congress supported the overall mission of the program yet was faced with other budget requests and crises. Funding was not able to be continued at the levels sought for. Before the program was up and running, as early as

May 1956, the NPS found that the 1958 projections exceeded funding authorizations, prompting Region II director Howard Baker to manage the park superintendents' expectations by sending them a memo stating, "Not all needs can be met during the first few years of the Mission 66 program…it would take until 1966 to accomplish our goals."[13] Indeed, it took until 1972 to complete the extended program, known as Parkscape USA.

Rallying for Public Support

The public had brought attention to the parks crisis, and its support would prove critical to implementing and sustaining Mission 66. To this end, the Park Service responded to the loudest calls for action, perceived as the need to address overcrowding, improve physical facilities (for both public and staff), increase staff and conserve the precious natural resources in the service's care. The latter was a primary driver and selling point. Expansion of the interpretive programs and removal of improvements from the natural resources—along with thoughtful planning—were intended to satisfy these concerns. Promulgation of the ideals—both within the Park Service and without—proved to be relatively easy when Mission 66 was first introduced.

The first initiatives were directed to all Park Service employees before there even was an official Mission 66. Wirth sent an informational memorandum to the Washington and other field offices in March 1955, asking for their input. He wrote, "Each employee who feels he has something to contribute to the Mission is urged to submit his personal views (regardless of area or subject) directly to the Committee without regard to normal channels of official communication."[14] Employees were also treated to slideshow presentations. These actions had two aims: to get employee ideas and buy-in and to educate employees who were typically the face of the Park Service to visitors. The Mission 66 Advisory Committee distributed question-and-answer booklets to all personnel, providing them with the knowledge base to give talks in campfire programs and other venues. The Advisory Committee stressed, "One of the best places to sustain interest in Mission 66 is in the impressive setting of the parks where people are in a receptive frame of mind."[15]

Visitors were targeted by park literature and signs; advertisements on television, radio and newspaper; newspaper and magazine articles; and films. Newspapers included editorials and letters supporting the program.

Committee members asked "interested and influential men" such as Herbert Hoover and Alfred Knopf to be ambassadors "to assist in furthering the objectives of Mission 66."[16] Wirth's political acumen also included authoring a series of articles in various publications, prompting others to do so and making television and radio appearances. If this were a present-day program, he would surely have created an app for it, a QR code and a blog.

Max Gilstrap wrote a series of thirty articles in the *Christian Science Monitor* that spanned from September 1955 to May 1956. Gilstrap's first article introduced the program to the public before it had federal funding—reaching as he said "a massive effort by the National Park Service—backed by expected public and congressional support—has been launched to provide over a 10-year period urgently needed personnel and facilities for mounting hordes of visitors to 180 park service areas." He spoke of the "rising wind of public concern over repeated reports of its inadequate services," emphasizing that "its success will depend largely on the budgetary support the service can get from Congress."[17] Gilstrap's last article, in May 1956, compelled the public to do its part to preserve the parks. Referring again to the "massive effort" to save the national parks, he invoked that "only an aroused and vocal public—the people who own the parks—can insure that the parks and monuments will be saved." And in summarizing the Park Service's briefing of the public, Gilstrap quoted Howard R. Stagner, assistant chief of the Mission 66 staff, as saying, "The program will go forward only so long as the American people are actively behind it."[18] Wirth delivered the final article of the series, referring to Mission 66 as a conservation program that would lessen impairment of the parks.

Not surprisingly, the tour bureaus of the petroleum companies, such as Sinclair Oil Corporation and Phillips 66, published advertisements and brochures that provided maps and images of the parks and spoke of how Mission 66 was making it all more enjoyable for everyone. *Your National Park System: A Passport to Adventure*, presented by Phillips Petroleum Company in 1964, was a picture book that explained the history of the Park Service, highlighted several of the parks and described the importance of Mission 66. The introduction by the new NPS director, George B. Hartzog Jr., spoke of the Park Service's mandate "to manage the superlative natural, historical and recreational areas that comprise your National Park System."[19] This coincided with Secretary of the Interior Stewart Udall's 1964 report that the parks needed to be managed within these three area types.[20]

Such advertising continued throughout the term of Mission 66 yet never matched the intensity of the early years. As early as 1958, the Park

Service identified the difficulty of getting feature articles about Mission 66 published. They found that the story was considered old news and that it was "difficult to present new ideas or approaches so that the stories could have fresh appeal." Local media limited coverage to the opening of park improvements in their areas, particularly if NPS officials attended dedication ceremonies. It was agreed that feature writers would develop new approaches themselves if they spoke with Park Service employees directly and that "supermarket magazines, which reach millions of readers, should not be overlooked."[21]

Chapter 3

MISSION 66

DISSEMINATED BY MEMORANDA

Within the limitations of the fundamental objectives of the National Park Service to protect and preserve, the lid is off.
—Conrad L. Wirth, March 17, 1955

Instructional Memoranda No. 2, quoted above, was part of a series of effective communication efforts by Wirth to disseminate the merits and methods of Mission 66. Wirth distributed these memoranda, at a fast pace, to the Washington office and all field offices. The following chronological synopsis sums up Wirth's, and the Steering Committee's, intentions for this huge undertaking called Mission 66.

The first of these memoranda was issued on February 18, 1955. Wirth explained the need for Mission 66 and the current objective of presenting the program for funding. He'd authorized a working staff to implement the instructions of the Steering Committee, relieving staff of their regular duties until the intensive study of all park operations was completed. He advised the use of imagination and vision, asking for new outlooks to the old issues. This became a common theme throughout the program. He stressed, "Because of the urgency of the project, I am initiating it immediately."[22]

In Memoranda No. 2, dated March 17, 1955, Wirth attached a questionnaire that the Steering Committee and staff had prepared, hoping to elicit response from Park Service people everywhere. He stated the overarching tenets simply:

Those working on Mission 66 are under instructions to:
1. *Disregard precedents.*
2. *Be imaginative in considering all problems to the end that ideas may be produced which are worthy of adoption.*
3. *Bring up something effective in achieving the twin objectives of protection and optimum use.*[23]

Each park was asked to review its visitor load and use and intrusion on the park's values and to propose solutions to the associated problems. The analysis of these answers was to be combined with any master plans, as updated to address the ramifications of automobile travel and overnight accommodations. These exercises were to be the backbone of each park's prospectus, to be submitted to the Steering Committee for review. Wirth demanded that removal of encroachment on "precious areas" be an established policy, citing that action was already underway in several parks. "In Yellowstone the Canyon development is being moved back from the Rim." The Park Service would work with the concessioners to locate new development at the "lesser areas." Even the Old Faithful hotel and lodge in Yellowstone were to be moved.[24]

While Wirth continued to insist on originality, he paired this premise with a reminder of the origins and purpose of the Park Service, which were still applicable and sound. An unnumbered informational memorandum, dated March 21, 1955, was a cover sheet for prior Secretary of Interior Franklin K. Lane's policy to the first NPS director, Stephen T. Mather, in 1918. Wirth included Lane's statement as proof that their agenda was still based on its principles.

In Instructional Memorandum No. 3, dated June 27, 1955, Wirth identified eight parks selected for pilot studies. The pilot parks were intended to be representative of all the parks. Mount Rainier and Yellowstone were at the top of the list. Each of the chosen parks was to submit a prospectus to the Steering Committee by July 20, 1955. The submissions were to address protection, development, interpretation and operation. The committee's suggested revisions were to be incorporated by July 31. This tight schedule was only possible because the parks had been primed for this and the Park Service dedicated staff to the effort. The attached guiding principles for the pilot studies noted the expectation that private enterprise would play an active role in this endeavor. This is where the park's concessioners—such as the Yellowstone Park Company—would be asked to step up and finance developments in new areas of the parks, abandoning prior developments in which they had already invested heavily. The level of concessioner financial commitment in Mission 66 vastly exceeded prior levels—enough so that in September 1955 the Park Service tried, unsuccessfully, to establish a revolving loan fund to assist the concessioners.[25]

Yellowstone was one of the few parks mentioned specifically in Wirth's informational memoranda, as Wirth had begun discussions with the park superintendent and the primary accommodations concessioner as early as 1953. Despite this communication, Yellowstone's superintendent, Edmund B. Rogers, failed to grasp that the instructions from the third memorandum applied to Yellowstone; he expressed disappointment that the pilot study for Yellowstone would not be reviewed with six other pilot parks in September. Rogers had not submitted a prospectus for Yellowstone, believing that the pilot parks were excused from doing so. Regional Director Howard Baker had concurred, feeling that this seemed like a lot of duplication. This situation appears to have resolved itself, as Yellowstone's Canyon area became the focus project, primarily because NPS's contract with the concessioner was due to expire at the end of 1955.

FROM PILOT TO INAUGURAL

Conrad Wirth had been planning ahead. He had contacted the Yellowstone hotels concessioner, the Yellowstone Park Company (YPC), in December 1953. His direct communication expressed interest in the Canyon and Lake developments, without showing priority for the Canyon area. In May 1955, he delayed negotiations for the concessioner's new twenty-year contract—which would include planning for several areas in Yellowstone—because he wanted "to combine the discussion of contract terms with an adequate and sound development program…I feel so strongly on the point of development that a firm commitment on it should be incorporated in any new contract that may be granted." His veiled threat that this would be true "regardless of who may be authorized to provide public accommodations" was continued in subsequent letters to YPC, proposing that perhaps NPS would engage a different concessioner for each tourist center in the park and thus infuse more capital into the Park.[26] At this time, Wirth stated that the Canyon development plan was established.

Wirth and the Steering Committee reviewed the pilot and master plans of the eight parks, singling Yellowstone National Park out because the concession contracts (for Yellowstone Park Company and Hamilton Stores) were up for negotiation. This presented an "opportunity to make sure the plans of the concessionaires and those for the park itself would be in harmony." In early 1955, Wirth and the Mission 66 staff committee hosted a weeklong meeting with Yellowstone's superintendent, landscape architect, chief ranger and chief naturalist in D.C. to study the Park's master plan.[27] The importance of the Canyon Village project at Yellowstone to the entire Mission 66 program cannot be understated; it was important that the project be successful and that Mission 66 start off on a positive note. This was conveyed, by National Park Service associate director E.T. Simpson, to Yellowstone's superintendent in March 1956, soon before construction of Canyon Village was to begin: "At Canyon, your high priority projects are nearly complete and we are using the development of your area as an example of the way we hope to do things in more places, not only in Yellowstone but in other areas of the System."[28]

The Park Service was heavily depending on the success of a project still in the planning stages, hoping to use this aspect of the Canyon Village project as part of the example. The Mission 66 Advisory Committee recommended in May 1956 "that a progress movie with sound track be produced this year of a typical Mission 66 development, such as at the Canyon area in Yellowstone, showing 'before' and 'after' conditions, and an 'on the job' story of continuity from the work of site selection, survey, planning, layout, and final building to the use of the new facilities."[29]

The Canyon Village project was similar to several others in the Park system in that its planning predated Mission 66. When the final Yellowstone prospectus was issued in November 1955—by the November 15 deadline—it reflected the top priority status held by Canyon Village, noting that this new village center was conceived in 1935 and progress had been interrupted by the war. The government would provide the site and road improvements and government facilities—visitor center, utility buildings, campgrounds and the like—and the concessioner would provide a cabin office, laundry and showers; a cafeteria, a coffee shop and a lounge; and a recreation hall, dormitories and employee housing, 750 cabin rooms, a service station and a garage. The prospectus included a series of charts demonstrating increased park visitation from 1932 to mid-1954 (and projections to 1970) and allocation of hotel and cabin rooms, campgrounds and trailer courts designed to accommodate the increased pillow count. The Park itself planned to spend $487,500 at Canyon in 1956, $911,200 in 1957 and $239,300 in 1958, for a total expenditure of $1,843,400 (with no explanation of why the three years of expenditures didn't add up to the total). In an accompanying document, the Park stated an estimated government expenditure of $55 million over the next ten years and private capital investment of $15 million.[30] Each year of Mission 66 brought planning changes, with each park issuing a new prospectus, adjusting priorities and increasing budgets.

Updating the Concessions Contract

Conrad Wirth's direct communications with both the Yellowstone Park superintendent and concessioner YPC reflected the need for the concessioner support to build this new business model. Mission 66 could not be accomplished without the concessioners and their lending institutions. Both Hamilton Stores and YPC had made funding projections in 1952, based on plans reviewed by the Park Service. YPC's post–World War II spending for capital investments and repairs had averaged $500,000 per year; YPC was hoping to reduce that to $335,000 per year. These amounts were financed by the concessioners without the encumbrance of loans. The Canyon development promoted by the Park Service in 1955 changed the whole outlook for YPC. This larger, more extensive project would cost $3 million, causing YPC to question whether it would be compensated for the buildings taken out of commission at the existing settlement closer to the Canyon rim and to also consider if it wanted any part of this. While the project was occurring at a fast pace already—design had begun in September 1955—in keeping up with Mission 66, the contract negotiations hit several snags; the contract was not signed until February 3, 1956, constricting the timeline needed for the April 1, 1956 construction start date. The $3 million bank loan was secured on March 30, 1956.

YPC had agreed, in an August 31, 1955 letter to the Park Service, that "an orderly program of expansion of the existing facilities" was warranted, if the expansion provided "profit sufficient to amortize the loan with a reasonable return to the stockholders." (YPC did not mention that all the stockholders were family members.) William Nichols of YPC stated that it needed a firm contract with the Park Service before December 31, 1955, and offered to meet with NPS in D.C.[31] Nichols's request for a meeting in June had fallen through, and he was anxious to get everything in place before securing funding. YPC's accountant stressed this latter point again to NPS's assistant director in mid-September, suggesting a meeting in the Park sometime after October 15.[32] YPC and its accountant finally met with NPS in Washington to finalize and sign the contract on October 28, 1955, agreeing to spend $3.5 million on the Canyon Village and Lake area improvements over the first ten years and $13.1 million within fourteen years.[33] It was anticipated that the Park Service would submit the contract for review by Congressional committees within the required sixty-day period; the contract received committee approval on December 1 and was forwarded to Congress. Yet the House Committee on Interior and Insular Affairs scheduled hearings to review the contract in a special session—to which the concessioners were not invited. Congressmen Hill (Colorado) and Thomsen (Wyoming) had requested this additional step in opposition to the contract "because Governor Simpson of Wyoming had taken it upon himself to complain present facilities in the Park were inadequate, outmoded, etc."

Governor Milward L. Simpson's complaint was not new and represented an insightful understanding of the issues at hand, citing the need to catch up on maintenance backlogs and that the funding level would not be adequate. Simpson had stated back in September 1955 that the $2.3 million [*sic*] concession contract was not sufficient justification for another twenty-year contract, adding that it was "merely a token… we need five times that much improvement and expenditure of a million dollars a year to catch up and stay up with park improvements to meet the expanding tourist needs." He was pleased to see an effort being made, with the federal government paying for new sewer and water systems, emphasizing that it should have been done years before.[34] Of greater significance, however, was that Simpson had also proposed that Wyoming should purchase and run the park concessions, starting with YPC's. The governor released a report (from an independent Chicago financial appraisal firm) of the concession facilities that endorsed state purchase as "fundamentally sound because it affords an opportunity to all parties to attain legitimate and beneficial objectives." It was opined, as reported in the *Billings Gazette* on September 9, 1955, that the revenues would be invested back in the park facilities (rather than private hands) for capital improvements. The appraisal noted, "It is the burden of the impending capital improvement program plus the great difficulty in securing adequate long-term financing that has been one of the primary reasons that the present owners…have sought to sell the business."[35] YPC had wanted to sell the company and release itself of these heavy financial burdens. It had met with what it termed a Wyoming "Authority," asking Wirth if he would approve a sale (he needed more information), yet Wyoming was only willing to offer $4 to $5 million for YPC, Hamilton

Stores and Haynes Inc. combined. The YPC board wanted $12 million for YPC alone. The deal was closed.[36]

The House committee did pass the contract, trusting the recommendations of the interior department. William Nichols and Trevor Povah (of Hamilton Stores), who had been allowed to attend and testify at the full hearing, went home assured of success. Yet on January 26, 1956, they learned that the Senate committee deferred action on the contract, needing time to consider Wyoming senators O'Mahoney and Barrett's suggestions that YPC be required to spend $10 million during the first twelve years of the contract, which YPC thought "ridiculous." YPC and its attorneys met several times with NPS at the end of January to work out a satisfactory supplement to the contract that obligated YPC no further. The contract was finally made official on February 3, 1956, leaving YPC little time to organize the largest construction project—and associated financing—of its fifty-five-year history in the Park.[37]

The March 30, 1956 loan arrangements made with Security-First National Bank in Los Angeles were based on the estimated need for $3 million to make the improvements at Canyon Village. The original contract included construction of three hundred motel units, three dormitories, the main lodge building, Administration Building and a recreation hall. Work on the construction drawings proceeded in earnest at this point, and documents for the cabin fabrication were issued on April 9, 1956. The final cost would ultimately be $5.6 million, for a reduced scope of work.

The Yellowstone Concessioners

The three primary concessioners who partook in the Canyon Village development were longtime concessioners in the Park: Yellowstone Park Company (since 1901), Hamilton Stores (since 1915) and Haynes Photo Shops (since 1883). All three were family-owned companies that had learned to work and play with one another and to make money under increasingly different and expanded contractual terms with the government. Expectations for growth after a period of stagnation affected all three concessioners. The brief histories provided here are in descending order of the financial commitments required by each firm.

Yellowstone Park Company

The Yellowstone Park Company (YPC) is the descendant firm of several concessions that Harry Wilbour Child's family held in the Park. The firm adapted in response to new Park management ideas, new modes of travel and a changing world. Such flexibility allowed it to prosper for years, yet did not prepare it for the enormity of what Mission 66 would require. YPC began in 1891 when Harry Child, his brother-in-law Silas Huntley and friend Edmund Bach were awarded the concession to provide transportation in the Park, replacing—and buying out the stock (stagecoaches, tack and horses) of—an earlier operation. In 1901, they used this firm (the Yellowstone Park Transportation Company) as collateral to purchase the Yellowstone Park Association (YPA). Additional financial support for this transaction came from the Northern Pacific Railroad, which brought tourists to the Park and thus would benefit from hotel development in the Park. In 1903, the railroad completed its branch line from Livingston down to Gardiner, by the north entry to the Park. The Yellowstone Park Association constructed Old Faithful Inn in 1903–4, the Mammoth (National) Hotel additions and extensive remodelings in 1911 and 1913 and the Canyon Hotel in 1911. The Canyon Hotel would be demolished in 1959–60, when structural remediation was determined to be too costly.[38]

By 1907, Huntley had died, Bach had lost his share of the company and Child had bought the remaining shares, giving him full ownership of YPA. He bought and developed other firms in the Park to lessen competition and bring the various offerings into one family of businesses. When Child died in 1931, his heirs received four companies: the Yellowstone Park Transportation Company, the Yellowstone Park Hotel Company, the Yellowstone Park Boat Company and the Lodge and Camps Company. In 1936, his wife, Adelaide; daughter, Ellen; and son-in-law, Billie Nichols, consolidated the four entities into the Yellowstone Park Company, easing financial oversight. The family remained in the business, bringing on other family members. Billie Nichols's son, John Q. Nichols, and his nephew, Huntley Child Jr., became officers. Historian Mark Daniel Barringer provided a concise summary of the complex company structure, which was crafted by the family's trusted accountant, Hugh D. Galusha:

> *Galusha had helped Child construct…a complex financial structure to limit tax exposure. They established the H.W. Child Trust, a holding company owned by family members, including Adelaide, daughter Ellen*

> *and her husband, Billie Nichols, their children (John, Dean, and Adelaide Nichols), and another grandchild, Huntley Child Jr. The trust retained forty thousand shares of the H.W. Child Corporation, which owned the Yellowstone Park Companies. The family trust also owned nearly two-thirds of the Vernon Goodwin Company, still nominal proprietor of the Lodge and Camps Company.*[39]

The Yellowstone Park Company was configured in this fashion at the time of the Mission 66 contractual negotiations, as well as throughout the remaining duration of the firm. The family trust was to be protected, as "the family has always been sensitive about any involvement of the H.W. Child Corporation either with the government or anyone else. This will mean that the Yellowstone Park Company will have to be the only obligatory and the collateral will have to be limited to the collateral of Yellowstone Park Company. Limits the collateral to $713,440."[40] Through the course of the Mission 66 projects, and its increasing monetary commitments, YPC's fears that the loans would never equal the financial gains were realized. YPC struggled to hold on to the firm. Billie and his son, John Q. Nichols, stepped aside in the early 1960s, leaving management in the hands of outsiders. They lost financial control, and as they realized they would not be able to fulfill the terms of their twenty-year contract, their alternate attempts to reorganize or sell the company resulted in the 1966 transfer to the Goldfield Corporation. Goldfield sold the firm a few months later to General Baking, which became General Host Inc. in 1967. General Host was also unable to comply with the Park Service contract, which was subsequently terminated in 1976. TWA Services, now Xanterra Parks & Resorts, was awarded the concession contract in November 1979. These transactions illustrate the challenges of such contracts, which Xanterra has proven capable of addressing. The Park Service awarded Xanterra a new twenty-year contract in February 2013. The contract covers lodging, retail sales and restaurant operations in the Park—and specifically includes the enhancement of Canyon Village Lodge, the companion Administration Building and new lodges (as replacement to the Mission 66 cabin lodging).[41]

Hamilton Stores

Hamilton Stores was formed by Charles A. Hamilton ("Ham") in 1915, with a $300 loan from Harry Child. The loan enabled him to purchase the Klamer Store at Old Faithful. His success encouraged him to enter into the service station business with Child, taking advantage of the increased automobile traffic in the Park. His second store, by the shore of Yellowstone Lake, was his first new construction. This octagonal wooden structure has a soaring interior with one storage and three retail wings. He cut his business teeth on these stores—using local burled wood, rhyolite stone and obsidian sand—and learned to deal (albeit sometimes gruffly) with the NPS officials who dictated work schedules, construction practices and colors. Ham went on to acquire and build more stores throughout the Park, as well as acquire other concessioners. Historian Robert Goss summed up Ham's success neatly:

> *When Charles Hamilton took over the business in 1915, the "modern age" in Yellowstone was at hand. Motorized vehicles were allowed on the roads that year and took over completely in 1917, allowing faster and more comfortable travel, easier transport of materials and supplies, and eliminated the necessity of grazing cattle and horses on park meadows. Visitation doubled in 1915, and with the exception of the war years, dramatically increased on a yearly basis. By the time Hamilton died in 1957, visitation approached close to 1.5 million a year.*[42]

Hamilton Stores provided merchandise for the daily visitors, as well as the campers, who were coming in greater numbers. Ham's success was considered exceptional and one that he passed on to his son-in-law, Trevor Povah, who was cut of the same cloth, thus well prepared for dealing with concession contracts and senators. Povah became vice-president in 1948 and president upon Ham's death on May 28, 1957. In the 1950s, when Canyon Village was constructed, Hamilton Stores was experiencing its third period of expansion. With its 1953 purchase of the Pryor & Trischman stores at Mammoth and Canyon, Hamilton Stores became the sole general store business in the Park. In 1967, it purchased Haynes Photo Shops (and its nineteen Park stores) from Isabel Haynes.[43] On December 31, 2002, Hamilton Stores' eighty-seven-year business in the Park ended. A fifteen-year general store concession contract was awarded to Delaware North Companies in 2003.

Haynes Picture Shops

Historically, the public's first view of Yellowstone came from photographers visiting the site during the first expedition in 1870. Commercial photographers provided images—often three-dimensional stereoscopic ones—that opened up dreams of travel to those who viewed Yellowstone as an unapproachable land of geysers overrun by Native Americans. This heritage of democratizing the Park was embraced by Frank J. Haynes, whose images advertised the Park and helped transform it into a tourist mecca. Haynes's postcards have told the visual and appealing story of Yellowstone National Park since he first came to the Park in 1881. Hired as a photographer for the Northern Pacific Railway in 1875, he understood the advertising potential of the postcard. When he moved his photography studio to the Park in 1883, he became known as the Park's official photographer. Receipt of a ten-year lease of four acres each in the Upper Geyser Basin and Mammoth Hot Springs—with permission to construct the buildings required to develop photographs and sell them to tourists—was the beginning of a long-held hold on the images taken of the Park. He produced his first set of postcards in 1900. Haynes ultimately had shops at all the major Park sites: Old Faithful, Mammoth, Canyon, Fishing Bridge, Lake, West Thumb, Tower and Roosevelt. One of Haynes's greatest contributions to the history of Yellowstone was his nearly annual publication, *Haynes Guide: Yellowstone National Park*. Published from 1890 until 1966, the book provides snapshots of nearly every year of Yellowstone history, marking the changes in maps and area descriptions.

Frank's son, Jack Ellis Haynes, became his partner, taking over the business in 1916. Jack grew up in Mammoth and spent most of his life in the Park, enjoying the moniker "the Postcard Man." He dedicated much of his time and interest in later life working with historian Aubrey L. Haines on the history of Yellowstone.[44] Frank died in 1921, and Jack Ellis died in 1962. Jack's wife, Isabel, continued the business, eventually selling it to Hamilton Stores in 1967. The stores are currently managed by Delaware North Companies as general stores or adventure stores (as is the case at Canyon Village).

Haynes had a photo shop in Bozeman, Montana, which it operated during the winter. This likely was the introduction to local architects Fred Willson and his successor, Bill Grabow. In 1959, Jack Haynes hired Grabow to design the new Haynes Photo Shop at Canyon Village and enlarge and remodel the shop at Tower Falls.

The Same Boat

Both YPC and Hamilton Stores had expressed the same (verbatim) concern about financing the Mission 66 projects, stressing the need for assured financial success of the new developments. Both William (Billie) Nichols and Charles Hamilton shared their identical concern in separate letters to Edmund Rogers, YNP's superintendent, in June 1956:

> *We have found that our own confidence in Yellowstone Park is shared to a degree, by certain financial institutions who have agreed to finance the current expansion program. However, in order to obtain this financing, it was necessary for us to demonstrate that there was sufficient earning capacity in the Company as a whole to protect the loan agencies in the event the anticipated revenue at Canyon Village did not materialize or prove to be less than anticipated...It has been made perfectly clear to us by these loan agencies (and, I am sure, is clear to you) that further expansion in Yellowstone Park, however desirable at a particular moment, will be conditioned upon our being able to demonstrate to these people a sufficient earning capacity to repay further loans...In short, we have been told, we cannot expect to borrow money to the limits of optimum profits but must always provide to our creditors a reasonable margin to protect them against temporary earnings shrinkages, however caused.*[45]

The passing of the old guard occurred between the June 24, 1956 groundbreaking and the August 31, 1957 dedication of Canyon Village Lodge. Both Billie Nichols and Charles Hamilton wielded shovels at the first event yet were in the ground for the second. Charles Hamilton died, in his apartment at Old Faithful, on May 28, 1957. Billie Nichols died on August 6, 1957. Jack Ellis Haynes enjoyed the opening of his new Canyon store in 1960 before his passing in 1962. Each of these patriarchs, entrepreneurial mavens in unchartered territory, left family to continue their legacies. Trevor Povah, husband of Hamilton's daughter, Ellie, had been the firm's vice-president and skillful NPS contract negotiator since 1948. John Q. Nichols remained with YPC until the 1966 sale, and Jack Haynes's wife, Isabel, sold the Haynes Photo Shops to Hamilton Stores in 1967.

THE PRIVATE ARCHITECTURAL FIRMS WHO DESIGNED CANYON VILLAGE

Due to the nascence of the program and fast pace of the Canyon Village project, private architecture firms were commissioned for all of the buildings for the three concessioners, as well as the Park Service. Later Mission 66 projects would have more initial design input by NPS's architects; for Canyon Village, NPS architects instead were limited to a strong review role. The NPS architects—YNP's landscape architect Frank Mattson and WODC's supervisory architect Lyle E. Bennett—met several times with the private firms hired by the concessioners, and their reviews affected the final designs.

Welton Becket & Associates

The firm responsible for designing the site layout and the buildings for YPC and Hamilton Stores was Welton Becket & Associates (WB&A). YPC, which did not have previous experience working with WB&A, selected the firm prior to YPC's contract renewal with NPS, hoping to gain ground on the construction. At the time, WB&A had offices in Los Angeles, San Francisco, New York City and Kansas City, Missouri, and employed two hundred persons, of which twenty-eight were licensed architects, twenty-seven were licensed engineers (mechanical, structural, electrical and civil) and eighty-five to ninety-five were draftsmen. Each of these employees was selected "with consummate care," with the realization that "the organization could only be as good as its individual members."[46] The firm advertised its expertise in budget analysis, specifications, traffic, parking, architecture, estimating, research, kitchen layout, field supervision, merchandising, fixturing, illumination and multiple other disciplines. Despite the firm's large size, Welton Becket participated in the initial planning stages of all the projects, which ranged in type from professional buildings to shopping centers, hotels, site planning, restaurants and retail stores. Although it had not designed in the national parks before, it had designed large government buildings for the U.S. Navy and the U.S. Air Force, and it excelled in every type of project that was required for Canyon Village: hotel, restaurant, parking, retail and housing.

WB&A had won awards for the General Petroleum (1949) and the Prudential Insurance Buildings (1950) in Los Angeles. For the latter, WB&A had pioneered the use of modular wall design, an experience that most likely aided in the design of the Canyon Village cabins. WB&A's hotel designs were also deemed appropriate experience since they were essentially "complete communities since they include residential and recreation areas, shops, restaurants and central utility plants."[47]

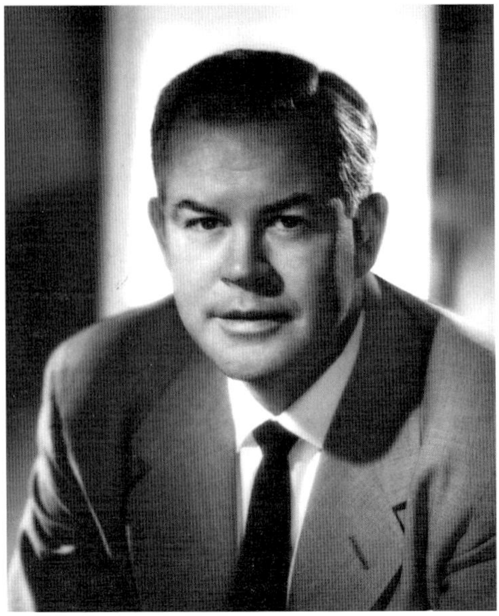

Welton David Becket, circa 1960. *Courtesy Bruce Becket.*

WB&A was known to have revolutionized department store design, resulting in an expanded client base that included Gimbels, Macy's, Orhbach's, Carson-Pirie-Scott, Bullock's, Joseph Magnin and Hart-Albin, to name just a few listed in its circa 1954 firm brochure. Yet it was likely Becket's moniker of "Mr. Shopping Center"—after having worked on twenty-one large suburban centers—that brought him to the attention of the Yellowstone Park Company. The Stonestown Shopping Center of San Francisco, completed in 1949, was a resounding success, with forty-eight stores and parking for 2,500 cars. The stores were carefully grouped around walking malls, away from the perimeter parking.

This multifaceted firm was led by Welton D. Becket, who was fifty-three years old and in his prime when engaged by YPC. His biography was well summarized in the *WB Reporter* (the firm's in-house publication) from the spring of 1969, which marked his passing on January 16, 1969:

> *Born Welton David Becket in Seattle, Washington, August 8, 1902, young Welton was drawn to architecture early in life since both his father and his 15-year-older brother Evro were builders. Following graduation from Queene Anne High School in Seattle, he entered the University of Washington, emerging in 1927 with a degree in architecture. This was followed by graduate study in architecture and fine arts at the Ecole de Beaux Arts in Fontainebleau, France. He entered the practice of architecture as chief designer for a Los Angeles firm in 1929, moved to Seattle two years later to practice on his own, and returned to Los Angeles in 1933 with classmate Walter Wurdeman, who passed away in 1949. Welton*

Becket and Associates was founded in 1949 as the succeeding firm to Wurdeman and Becket, and during the ensuing years, the firm grew from fewer than 50 employees to more than 500.[48]

Wurdeman and Becket had begun their practice with the established Los Angeles architect Charles F. Plummer in 1933 and gained recognition soon after for their award-winning design of the Pan Pacific Auditorium in 1935. This provided an introduction for them to the Hollywood scene and residential commissions for movie stars. Plummer died in 1939, after which the success of the firm Wurdeman & Becket continued to grow. After World War II, "Walt and Welt" were awarded sizeable commercial projects. As noted earlier, Wurdeman died in 1949, and Welton led the firm until his death in 1969.

The working philosophy of WB&A was described in its firm brochures and permeated in the *WB Reporter*, published internally from 1957 through 1986. "Total Design" was WB&A's self-proclaimed modus operandi:

The theory of "total design" is that one firm can best handle and harmonize all aspects of a job. It results in a completely integrated building and achieves savings. Total design means that the entire project—pre-design research, architecture, special fixtures, building colors and a multitude of details—is handled by one concern which has full perspective concerning the project, and its entire costs, as a whole. An original exponent of "total design," Welton Becket widened the design field to include, if desired, special fixtures such as tilted, hidden cash registers, symbolically-designed draperies, *special-purpose display cases and firm-crested chinaware.*[49] *In short, "Total Design" encompassed everything from "dishes to heavy construction."*[50]

William Dudley Hunt Jr. provided the more comprehensive definition from a later vantage point in his 1972 publication *Total Design: Architecture of Welton Becket and Associates*:

In its simplest terms, the phrase connotes both architectural philosophy and practice that embrace all of the services required to analyze any architectural problem, perform the necessary studies and research to solve the problem, and translate the solution into a building or group of buildings complete down to the last detail of furniture, sculpture and other art, landscaping, and furnishings, even to ashtrays, menus, and matchboxes.[51]

WB&A's two National Park Service projects—Canyon Village and Furnace Creek Visitor Center in Death Valley National Park with Cecil Doty (renowned NPS landscape architect stationed in the WDOC)[52] in 1959–60—were not mentioned in Hunt's publication, yet Canyon Village is included in its five-page "Index of Buildings" and illustrated in the body of the text. WB&A's large commercial projects—and, by translation, the Canyon Village project—were facilitated by WB&A's strong organizational and managerial structure, which enabled it to handle and track complex design and construction projects.

The Total Design approach—accompanied by hard work and a "liberal sprinkling of breaks, or good luck," as well as excellent relationships with repeat clients—helped WB&A grow into a large firm of more than five hundred employees with offices in Los Angeles (1939), San Francisco (1949), New York (1950), Houston (1960) and Chicago (1970).[53] Additional offices were established for specific projects in Dallas, Cairo, Cuba and Honolulu.

Welton Becket's nephew, architect MacDonald Becket, become president of WB&A in late 1968 and continued the firm's global growth throughout the 1970s and 1980s, shepherding the merger with Ellerbe Associates in 1987.[54] Ellerbe-Becket subsequently joined AECOM in 2009, fully transitioning as of May 2, 2011.[55]

WB&A's personnel most involved with the Canyon Village project were—from a conceptual level down to a detailed level—Welton Becket, Jack Beardwood, Gilbert Lord (project chief), Jack Campbell (designer), Dick Perkins (project architect), Ellis Kaplan and Tom Cole (specifications writer). Welton oversaw general design of the buildings and site. Jack Beardwood most likely brought the commission into the office and negotiated the contracts with YPC and Hamilton Stores. Gil Lord often met with WODC in San Francisco and established a presence on site. Ellis Kaplan was the on-site construction observation architect, who visited on an intermittent basis during construction and revised drawings as necessary.[56]

Welton Becket, age fifty-four in 1956, was well established in his career; he had been anointed a Fellow of the American Institute of Architects in 1951, "one of the youngest architects ever to receive this coveted honor."[57] He nurtured his client relationships, launched projects after the initial planning and then oversaw them from a bird's-eye viewpoint. He was not intimately involved in document production or the construction; none of the Canyon Village available project correspondence is from his hand. He did, however, attend the significant ceremonial events for the Canyon Village project.

Welton was a friend of Dwight Eisenhower—they frequently golfed together—and of motion picture stars. Welton's relationship with Eisenhower resulted in related commissions, or vice versa. WB&A designed the Eisenhower Foundation Building in Abilene, Kansas, which was opened to the public in the spring of 1954. Upon Welton's death in 1969, a warm tribute in the firm newsletter summed him up as follows: "He loved work, he loved play, he loved life. His was a rich life, a full life, a meaningful life."[58]

Jack Beardwood joined WB&A in 1953 (at age thirty-nine) as an executive assistant to Welton Becket, to develop business. He had strong managerial experience and a relationship with Dwight Eisenhower (which might have been how he came to WB&A). After serving in World War II, he served as chief of the press section in D.C. for the Citizens for Eisenhower campaign, which helped Eisenhower ascend to the presidency in 1953. Beardwood brought to WB&A "what may be an unprecedented architectural workload for any one man." He traveled around the United States and the world, introducing WB&A's qualifications to titans of industry and government. During his twenty-year tenure at WB&A, the firm staff size increased to four hundred, and the company established three wholly owned subsidiaries: Becket International, The Energy Group and Project Purchasing Services Inc. The number of master planning projects increased exponentially (reflecting the client need and WB&A's abilities), as did the number of commissions for government agency buildings (municipal, federal and international) and large institutional clients. Beardwood made sure that WB&A was considered for these commissions.[59]

In his role at WB&A, Beardwood was treated to what he referred to as the "quite salty" language of Charles Hamilton. His first conversation with Hamilton in January 1956, during which they discussed hiring WB&A for the design of Canyon Village Hamilton Store, was "quite delightful" and ended in mutual agreement to tell each other to "go to hell" if they couldn't reach an agreement.[60]

As project chief, architect Gilbert Lord managed the client relationship once the project had been awarded to WB&A. He met with NPS design staff at the WODC and at YNP, revised locations for the dormitories and cabins, addressed drawing deficiencies noted by YNP staff and brought his wife to the groundbreaking ceremony in June 1956.

Ellis Kaplan, who had attended Harvard Graduate School of Design after receiving an undergraduate degree in 1946, was a junior architect at WB&A in the mid-1950s. He was assigned to administer construction at Canyon Village, a task that involved a lot of learning—to communicate effectively and tactfully, respond and design on your feet and document the decisions. Frank Mattson expressed apparent surprise at Kaplan's role, indicating after a February 1956 review of the designs that "[h]e, incidentally, did the speaking for the Welton Becket firm."[61] Kaplan's initials on various WB&A Canyon Village drawings indicate that he was supervising the changes. In 1963, Kaplan, Jim Diaz and Herb McLaughlin formed the eponymous firm McLauglin Kaplan Diaz (MKD). The firm became a highly respected architectural firm in San Francisco, known as the city's first multiethnic all–Ivy League architecture firm with a Harvard Jew (Kaplan), a Yale Irishman (McLaughlin) and a Princeton Hispanic (Diaz). Kaplan died in October 2012.[62]

During the period of Canyon Village's design and construction, WB&A was working on the Broadway's twin department stores in the southern part of California, with an $8.5 million construction cost for each. The December 22, 1955 issue of the *Seminole Sentinel* described the impending construction of an ultramodern $25 million skyscraper Sheraton-Dallas Hotel designed by WB&A.[63] The firm was also designing the $1.3 million engineering facility for AIResearch next to the Los Angeles International Airport, as well as the Police Facilities Building in Los Angeles.[64] The firm was accustomed to designing and managing large complex projects.

WB&A are known to have designed one other national park project: the Furnace Creek Visitor Center in Death Valley National Park in 1959. This design was a cooperative project—as many visitor centers were—with NPS landscape architect Cecil Doty.

Hurt & Trudell Architects

Hurt & Trudell Architects of San Francisco designed the Canyon Visitor Center for the National Park Service. The drawings, prepared in September 1956 and updated in January 1957, provided for construction that was completed for the dedication in August 1958. Hurt & Trudell was an architecture firm led by principals Edgar Burton Hurt and Clyde Francis Trudell.

Clyde Trudell was born in San Francisco on December 25, 1905, and educated at Colorado University in 1927–29, after attending the Beaux Arts Institute of Design in New York from 1925 to 1927. After graduation, he was employed from 1929 to 1933 as an architect at the Rockefeller Restoration of Williamsburg, Virginia. He worked with the National Park Service

(Department of the Interior) from 1933 to 1938, had his own practice in San Francisco from 1938 to 1943 and then worked with the United States Navy Civil Engineer Corps from 1943 to 1946. He and Hurt formed their firm in 1948, designing buildings primarily for the navy and the air force, in addition to some school design.[65]

Trudell's work with the National Park Service and other federal agencies probably had bearing on the selection of his firm for the Canyon Visitor Center design. During his six years working with the National Park Service, he likely had become acquainted with Conrad Wirth, who had begun his long Park Service career there in 1931.[66] Hurt, Trudell & Capell also designed the visitor center at Craters of the Moon National Monument in 1956–58.[67]

William E. Grabow

Bill Grabow grew up in Livingston, Montana, a thriving town fifty-one miles north of the north entrance to Yellowstone National Park. After high school, he spent three and a half years in the U.S. Army. After World War II, he initiated his architectural education by touring Belgium and France, where he saw hundreds of cathedrals. From 1946 to 1950, he studied architecture at Montana State College. After graduation, he worked for Bozeman's prolific architect Fred Willson. Grabow's college instructors had promoted modern design, giving Grabow a comfort level with this genre that his employer did not have. Willson had worked with the Haynes family extensively over the years and with the Park, designing in the 1930s buildings for a new Canyon Village that was never constructed. When Willson died in 1956, Grabow took over his office and inherited the Haynes's commissions.

In 1958, when Grabow was designing the Haynes Photo Shop for Canyon Village, he was working jointly with Bozeman architect Ozzie Berg on the Bozeman high school. One year later, he designed a remodeling of the Tower Junction Photo Shop for Haynes, expanding the footprint and altering the once rustic design into a modern structure not unlike the new Canyon Photo Shop. Several of his projects entailed the application of a modern appearance to an older building, often originally designed by Willson.[68]

The National Park Service Personnel Who Monitored the Design of Canyon Village

The National Park Service's objective at Yellowstone was twofold: to supervise the design and construction work of others and to design and supervise construction of the site improvements and the new Canyon Visitor Center. This oversight was provided by Lyle E. Bennett in the WODC and Frank Mattson, Yellowstone's landscape architect. The Washington NPS office emphasized that Mission 66 was "largely a field program,"[69] clarifying that the Washington office and WODC would coordinate and advise and that the park's staff were responsible for planning and developing the projects.

Frank E. Mattson was born in 1901 and grew up in Minnesota. He received a landscape architecture degree from Iowa State University–Ames in 1931, when private design work was minimal, thus he was grateful to work for the National Park Service in the San Francisco office. He took part in the master planning process so prevalent at that time. He worked in Yellowstone the summers of 1932, 1934 and 1935 (1933 was spent in Grand Teton National Park), planning and supervising road and building construction. Frank was involved in the early planning stages of a Canyon Village, suggesting the facilities be located entirely away from Yellowstone's Grand Canyon rim. He continued his career with the National Park Service, leaving the regional office in San Francisco in 1934 and following a common pattern still extant today of working in several parks; he also worked in the Omaha regional office. After World War II, however, he became the resident landscape architect in Yellowstone, coordinating planning there, and at three other national parks: Grand Teton, Glacier and Custer Battlefield.[70] Frank played a strong role in directing the design of Canyon Village (and later Grant Village), urging it to be appropriate for the weather conditions, stylistic period and public perceptions. Frank remained in this role until he retired in the 1963.

Lyle E. Bennett was the supervising architect for the WODC in San Francisco during Mission 66. The office was directed by landscape architect Red Hill. The other landscape architect on staff, Robert G. Hall, does not seem to have been involved in the Canyon Village project, probably because of the strong and valued role of YNP landscape architect Frank Mattson.

Lyle Bennett received a degree in fine arts from the University of Missouri, where his primary study was architecture. There he developed a fine sensitivity for color, which he would draw on often in his career. After graduating, Bennett worked for the Park Service as a ranger in 1927 and

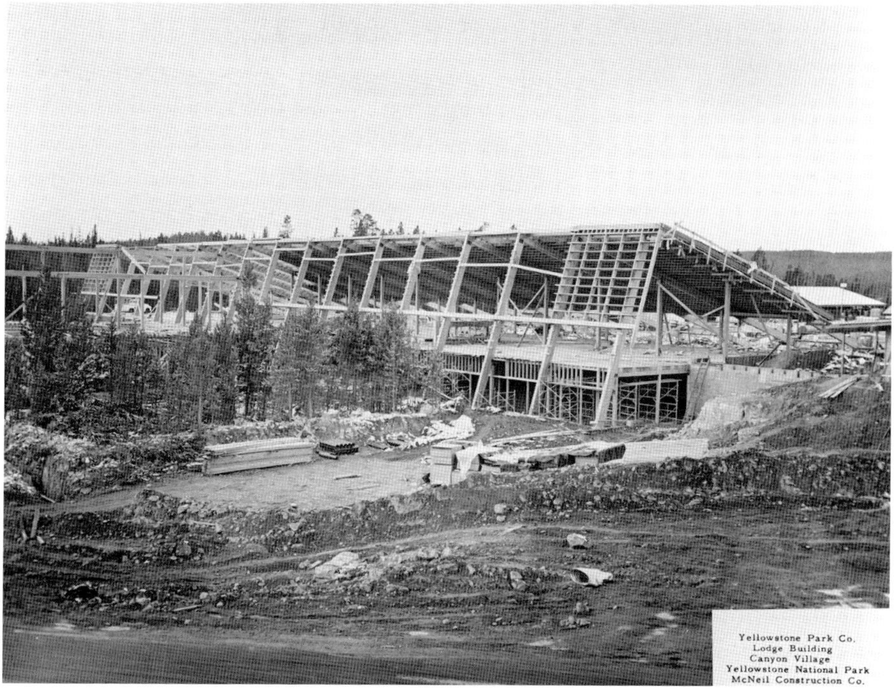

Canyon Village Lodge under construction, October 13, 1956. *Courtesy NPS, YNP, YELL 185385-59.*

designed buildings at Bandelier National Monument, Carlsbad Caverns, White Sands National Monument and Mesa Verde National Park. He was working out of NPS's Region II office in 1936 when he began designs for the highly regarded major rebuilding of the Painted Desert Inn in the Petrified Forest National Park (now a National Historic Landmark) and other park buildings in the rustic style.[71] The Park Service supervised the inn's construction by Civilian Conservation Corps (CCC) forces. As relayed by the CCC project superintendent, Bennett spent "hours at the site experimenting with color combinations and materials for paints and stains….The time I had personally spent with Mr. Bennett was a revelation to me of what can be accomplished with color combinations."[72]

Yet it was Bennett's application of his design expertise that proved critical to avoiding mistakes in what was a short period for design and construction of the Canyon Village project. His written reviews focused primarily on correct integration of mechanical and electrical systems and code compliance; it is hoped that his design expertise was offered during the early team meetings in San Francisco. He was involved in the master planning stages of Mission 66 projects and critiqued general design concepts. He also had a good relationship with WB&A and Mattson that seemed to circumvent the authorized chain of communication, causing YNP superintendent Lon Garrison to recommend that the internal lines of authority be clarified: "For example, we have a good project supervisor here, but the landscape architect and the architect assigned tend to clear their problems directly with their WODC Chief instead of through the [on-site] project supervisor [Al Heubner]."[73]

Chapter 4
THE DESIGN HISTORY OF CANYON VILLAGE

Architecture which is worthy of the name cannot readily be classified as utilitarian or monumental.
—Frank Mattson, YNP landscape architect

Location

Yellowstone National Park's planning for this site predated the Mission 66 program; it predated World War II and had been set aside in the wait for funding. In 1933, park planners proposed a new Canyon Village location outside what was known as the "sacred area." Prior development at the Grand Canyon of the Yellowstone had either encroached on or nearly abutted this zone, which had been redefined and yet ignored. The original legislation aimed to protect the significant features in the park—such as the Grand Canyon and the Old Faithful geyser—by preventing development within one-fourth of a mile of each feature. In 1935, this distance was reduced to one-eighth of a mile by those "less farsighted."[74] Mission 66 finally accelerated this relocation to a site that prevented misuse of the resource. The new site, two miles from the rim, was at a relocated Canyon Junction, requiring realignment of roads.

This new site also helped NPS control traffic, provide parking for the 500,000 cars that were coming through the park and room for the new list of expected amenities—in addition to giving a blank slate to the design team. What resulted was a village with a small shopping mall in a less attractive location compared to the dramatic falls, yet it resulted in a restored canyon rim.

It Takes a Village

Mission 66 would provide funding (for NPS), a vision and a tight schedule. NPS director Conrad Wirth needed to prove the worth and efficacy of the program. Wirth had not waited for presidential approval and legislative funding to start the planning. NPS had chosen Yellowstone's Canyon Village as a prototype in 1955, and design began that fall. As early as September 1955, the key players were in place. Yellowstone Park Company brought representatives of Welton Becket & Associates (WB&A) and McNeil Construction Company to the site to begin to develop design ideas and costs. The assistant director of NPS and NPS design chief Thomas Vint were at this meeting, setting the tone for the composition of the future team that would take this project on. Both NPS and the Yellowstone Park Company (YPC) were moving ahead without funding and without an updated concession contract.

All parties were working on the scope agreed on in earlier letters between Wirth and the YPC, reproducing and expanding the services provided at the existing Canyon rim development: a new main structure with a lobby, a dining room, a cafeteria and a kitchen to serve both; a separate recreation hall; and about three hundred rooms in new cabins. NPS would supply the roads and utilities.[75] This scope was maintained, with adjustments, throughout the course of the project.

The Horseshoe Shopping Plaza

Today, shopping malls are typically associated with crass commercialism, yet Canyon Village's offerings needed to be sold to the tourists—in order to feed and house them and to make it financially viable for the concessioners. Welton Becket & Associates brought extensive shopping mall, campus, hotel and retail experience to this project. The firm was also a large, efficient operation that was well poised to produce the required documents in the short time allotted.

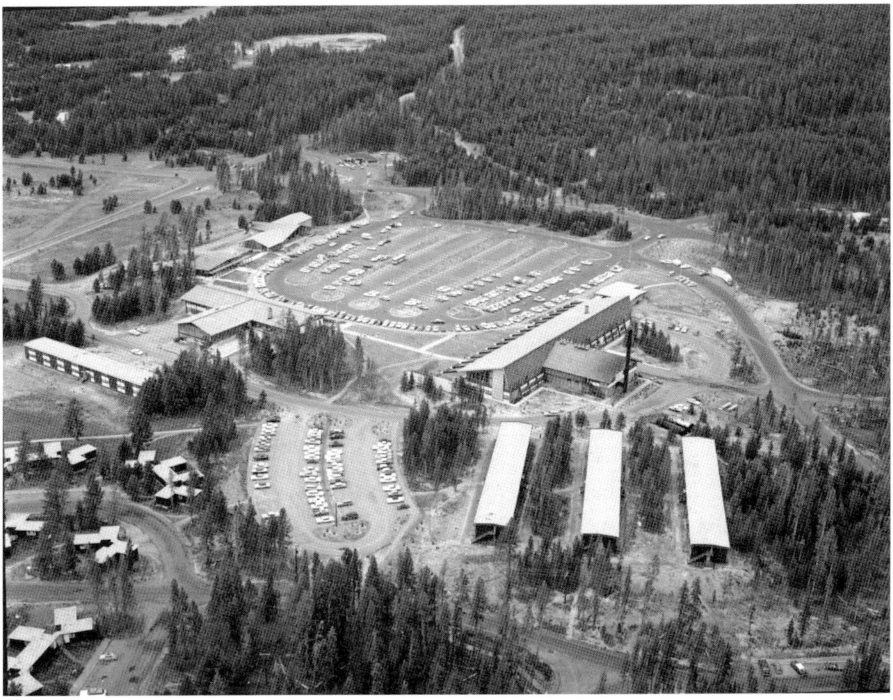

The horseshoe-shaped parking lot at Canyon Village provided central access to all the commercial buildings at the perimeter. Aerial photo looking northwest, 1963. *Courtesy NPS, YNP, YELL 27121.*

In the 1950s, a shopping mall was a modern piazza that separated concentrated parking from the pedestrian walkways. Becket's design here reversed his prior approach—and that of fellow L.A. designer Victor Gruen—of placing the buildings around a park, with car parking outside and separate. Gruen's concept in 1943 had been to construct a parklike plaza surrounded by restaurants, libraries and stores, making it "the center of cultural activities and recreation."[76] Becket's 1952 Stonestown Shopping Center continued this concept by placing the stores on either side of a landscaped pedestrian walkway. He was able to reverse that at Canyon Village because the natural park was outside the commercial area—it formed a lower, natural outside perimeter that paralleled the horseshoe-shaped parking plaza. Thus placing the parking in the center kept the sea of cars away from the Park and gave the visitors a grand, sweeping view of all the retail and cultural opportunities that encircled them.

The horseshoe plaza remains the core of the commercial area, accessed directly from an eastbound continuation of the Norris-Canyon Road. The intersection of Norris-Canyon Road and the Grand Loop Road became the new "Canyon Junction," from which one could travel north up Dunraven Pass to Tower and Roosevelt, southeast to the sites at the Grand Canyon or south to Lake and Fishing Bridge.

The Buildings

The primary day-use buildings encircled the Canyon Village parking area, in counterclockwise order as experienced from the west entry: NPS Visitor Center, Haynes Photo Shop, Hamilton Store, YPC's Canyon Lodge and YPC's Administration Building. From original planning until 1965, a place was held for YPC's Recreation Building between Hamilton Store and Canyon Lodge. The area outside the commercial circle[77] was dedicated to residential and utility buildings, including four identical dormitories and the cabins at each of three loop roads. The service station was located at the northeast corner of Canyon Junction for efficient automobile access. The laundry building for camper services is within the campground area east of the gas station.

To implement the Mission 66 mantra of eschewing precedent, NPS and the Park's concessioners engaged architects new to them and the Park experience. Welton Becket & Associates of Los Angeles designed the cabins, the plaza and all but two buildings around it. Another California firm, Hurt & Trudell Architects of San Francisco, was engaged to design the Park's Visitor Center, and Bozeman architect Bill Grabow designed the Haynes Photo Shop.[78]

The design process was guided by the NPS Building Construction Manual, which apparently was basically a code book. During a January 1958 meeting of YPC and NPS officials to review NPS policies, it was revealed that the manual was not updated to reflect current construction methods and materials, that many of the requirements were hard to comply with and expensive and that an insufficient number of manuals had been provided. The construction foremen weren't able to receive copies once YPC's six allotted copies had been distributed to the architects and engineers. The primary complaint against the manual, voiced here, related to color, a point of contention throughout the Canyon Village project:

> *The selection of colors for exterior use has always been a problem and many thousands of dollars have been spent repainting, recoloring or even*

> *re-ordering paint to obtain the colors requested by the Park Service. Such practice is costly and the concessionaires feel that some consideration should be given to an "easing of policy" whereby the use of more attractive and pleasing colors could be used instead of the somewhat drab and unattractive colors formerly required. Furthermore, the use of standard manufacturer's colors instead of special colors would be helpful.*[79]

The designs also reflected strong direction from the NPS. During the Mission 66 planning days, it had been determined that travel in the parks was now different than it was during the railroad days; more than 98.5 percent of visitors came in their own vehicles. This obviated the need for the large hotels of the early days because the tourists were staying in modern motels on their drives to the Park. It was believed that they would want similar accommodations in the Park itself. This aspect was well articulated in the January 1957 *Architectural Record* article about the Mission 66 program in which the system was called "a combination hotel and motel—motel in cabin or row-type sleeping rooms, hotel in dining and lounge facilities. So the public part of the hotel is built as a lodge building, which is surrounded by cabins or cottages."[80]

Building style had also been addressed in the instructions to all those working on Mission 66 projects (to be imaginative and to disregard precedents). With this direction, it is not surprising that YPC relied on Welton Becket to lead the charge. The firm's reputation for superb and functional design that fit within budget was a huge attraction. As with most projects, design changes occurred over the course of the fast-paced project due to several factors. Working in the Park was physically challenging, Park weather placed its own demands on structures and details, the architect and contractor had to satisfy both YPC managers and NPS officials and the understanding of what guests wanted and would pay for kept changing.

CANYON VILLAGE LODGE

WB&A's first designs for Canyon Village Lodge were issued in October 1955. Colored renderings illustrate the design intent and the soaring, expansive volume made possible by the use of glu-lam beams, which had become available for exterior use in 1942. Glu-lams were used more frequently in the mid-1950s, for their structural strength, fire resistance and warmth that steel could not provide. The early images are dramatic in the extensive use of glass (from floor to roof) and open space, two features that were drastically reduced in the final design. The glass reduction was most likely due to climate and the latter element to increased functional requirements—room for dining, the gift shop and so on. The final program for use of the public level of the building contained a spacious lounge with a bar, a gift shop, a dining room seating 250, a cafeteria seating 250, a lunch counter for 65 and restrooms. The building's T-shaped footprint remained consistent, with the main public area 320 feet long by 62 feet wide, and intersecting kitchen wing 70 feet wide by 86 feet long; the main interior volume soared to 27 feet. The main public space was contained under an eccentrically sloped gable roof, with a gentle, long (4:12) slope sliding toward the parking lot and the steep (12:3) slope diving down to the rear service yard. Other features were removed during the course of the project, primarily for budgetary reasons.

This initial design was reviewed thoroughly by the Park's landscape architect, Frank Mattson, who prefaced his comments to the Park superintendent: "Architecture which is worthy of the name cannot readily be classified as utilitarian or monumental." He stressed the paramount importance of aesthetics—particularly in this popular park, within this national context and the newness of this building program. He asked if it was "possible the objective overshadowed the more noble?"[81] His specific comments primarily addressed the design's lack of response to the conditions in the Park: snow conditions not being understood, the ridge needing to align with the southwest winds to prevent unbalanced snow load and steep roofs not always being the answer. He advised that the designer visit the site in early March.

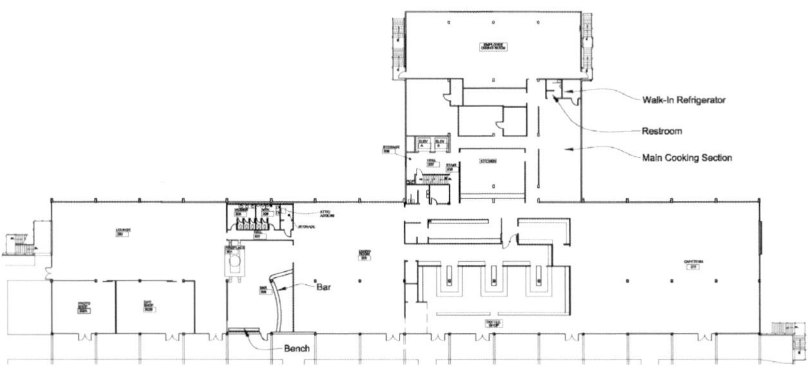

The 1956 floor plan of the main level of Canyon Village Lodge, as designed by Welton Becket & Associates. *Drawing by CTA Architects Engineers.*

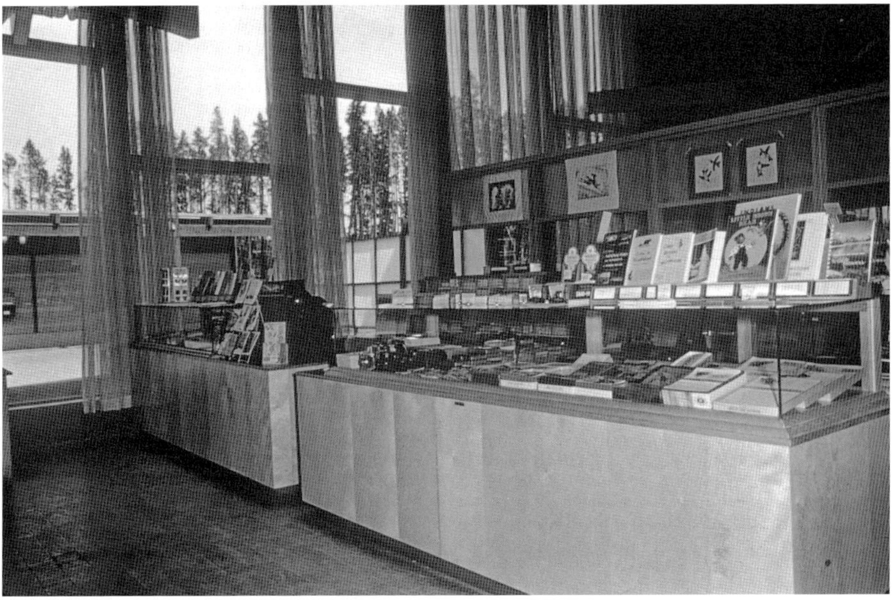

Temporary Haynes Photo Shop in the Canyon Village Lodge Gift Shop, looking northeast, 1957. The photo shop was inserted into the gift shop until the Haynes Shop was completed in 1960. *Photo by Haynes Studios Inc., courtesy of MHS RCPA Haynes Foundation Collection.*

The roof's visual aspects prompted equal comment: "The proportion of the roof which is one continuous plane and exposed to view is somewhat of a shock. This element apparently was in the minds of the others who said they were also shocked by the first look. First impressions are important for in these cases they generally hold the truth. The park visitor will also gain a first impression and that is the one they will take with them. In direct elevation 80% of the main is roof; in perspective it will be less."[82] The depiction of copper sheet roofing seemingly didn't concern Mattson in terms of snow slide but in terms of what color it would turn after aging—would it turn a dull neutral color (as shown in the rendering) or would it patinate to turquoise (which would not be acceptable)? Mattson also felt that the entry should be more obvious. The Park superintendent's monthly report for October 1955 indicated that he concurred, as he reported that the proposed plans for Canyon Village didn't fit well into the park scheme and needed a lot of changes.

Architect Gilbert Lord of WB&A, along with representatives of McNeil Construction, did visit the area in March 1956, yet it appears that they did not go to the Canyon site. They met in Gardiner (north of the Park) to review the pilot cabin structure but also discussed the finish for the glu-lam beams at the lodge. Mattson's experience in the Park again prevailed, as he explained that a transparent finish would require annual maintenance. It was agreed that the finish should be the same inside and outside.[83]

Newspaper coverage in May 1956 provided textural descriptions coincident with the anticipation of construction. The features shown in the renderings of the prior fall were included: the high gable roof, heavy timbers, sheer glass walls, some native stone veneer and copper roofs, in a contemporary design. The final construction documents, dated June 8, 1956, reflected revisions in the glazing, now to be set in a wood mullion system on a concrete base, set evenly within the twenty-foot structural bays; a wood shake roof; and the removal of two cost-saving items. The first, a reflecting pool, to be located at the north end of building and spanned by the covered walkway to the Administration Building, was now a planted area. Mattson did not comment on this pool, although it was shown in the early renderings and plans. This omission in the written record, of which Mattson was a master, relegates this impractical feature to a non-issue, one probably quickly dismissed verbally. The second cost-saving feature was found in the roofing selection. After construction was completed in August 1957, Mattson relayed relief when, after two other roofing materials were proposed (colored aluminum roofing and a built-up roof), WB&A proposed a shake roof, as it would "have a character that blends well with the site and helps tie the buildings to the ground."[84] Mattson also remarked that the lodge interior had been well received by the public and that the "interior decorations were excellent."[85]

The removal of a more practical component was documented by McNeil in an August 1, 1956 letter to YPC highlighting the items removed to reduce costs. The only lodge-related item was the mezzanine above the coffee bar. The earlier plans included a straight run of stairs across the north end of the coffee bar, up to what was to be a mezzanine with restrooms and a little mechanical space; a screen wall, similar to that at the gift shop, would have been lightweight and translucent. To save money, the stairs were omitted and the mezzanine volume remained, empty yet for a few duct runs. This large area, which connects to the attic over the kitchen wing, became a solid wall for decorative and colorful line art.

A November 1956 drawing revision cited as "remove reference to sculptured wood columns" (on detail sheet L-7-3) is the first reference to what appear to be carved wood columns in the early colored renderings. McNeil's job cost estimate from July 30, 1956, allocated a $5,000 cost for sculptured columns. In their stead, the single line of columns supporting the glu-lam beams are glu-lams as well.

Ornament in the lodge was sparse and thus noticeable against the backdrop of neutral wall and ceiling planes of clear finished narrow fir boards. The south and north end walls, of diagonally set fir boards, act as hearths, with further focus provided by decorative clocks. Line art, seemingly in homage to the American Indian,[86] covered two large wall areas: the west face of the mezzanine and the black-painted north wall of the dining room. These striking compositions were of thin, narrow boards, painted to contrast with their backgrounds, arranged in large-scale geometric patterns. The drawings make no mention of these diagrams, yet they appear in the early completion slides of the building.

Fortunately, a revision to the bar was accepted, as drawn in January 1957.[87] The footprint of the bar was reworked from a rigid L-shape to a gracious curve. Paired with the black-lit blue Miró-like mural above the back bar and the cove lighting above, the bar became a sophisticated oasis shielded by the massive fireplace and screen wall. Eight-foot-tall translucent screen walls were WB&A's sophisticated design solution to create differentiation of use and privacy without affecting the lodge's interior volume. A grid with evenly divided translucent panels set in wood mullions defined the bar, the gift shop and the lower-level beauty shops. Glass panes in the sliding doors and eye-height panel areas gave transparency where needed. In the 1970s, the north screen of the original bar area was removed. In the 1980s, the gift shop wall was extended to over ten feet (for security reasons), and all the panels were made opaque.

The lodge was originally designed to accommodate the public primarily on the main level, with a small portion of the lower level for visitor use. A barbershop, beauty salon and restrooms were located at the north end of the lower level, accessed by double doors at the base of the exterior stairway. The rest of the lower level was for employee housing, a large laundry, general and food storage and the boiler room. A loading dock was conveniently located at the northeast juncture between the two building wings. It was determined soon after opening that the public areas were too small, leading to conversion of the north half of the lower level from employee to communal use. This use would also generate income.

Thus the lodge was altered early to provide more income-producing spaces and more restrooms. In 1960, the lower-level laundry room was converted to meeting rooms, the north bedrooms into an employee recreation room—thus the showers in the restrooms could be converted into toilet stalls—and a

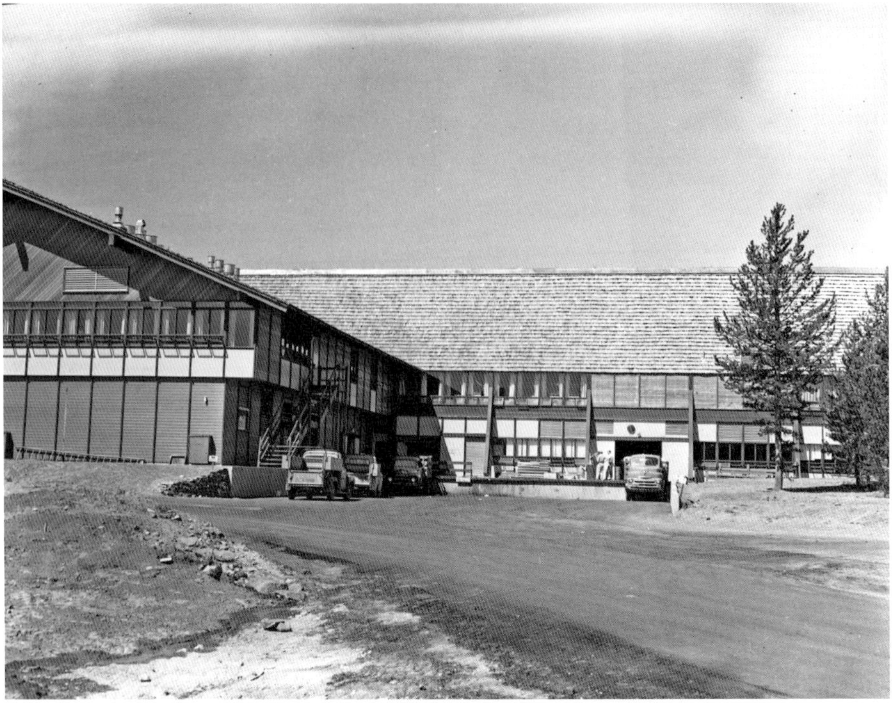

The loading dock at the northeast juncture of the two Canyon Village Lodge wings provided access to the laundry and kitchen storage facilities, August 1958. *Photo by Jack E. Boucher, courtesy of NPS, YNP, YELL 29672-10.*

stairway inserted up to the main level. Orr Pickering & Associates, a respected architectural firm in Billings, designed several versions of these modifications in 1959 and 1960. The July 31, 1959 plan located a C-shaped stairway immediately north of the main floor restroom block, leading down to a gracious foyer that accessed three large meeting rooms.[88] The final drawings, dated February 22, 1960, located a smaller stair in the northeast corner and replaced one of the meeting rooms with the employee pub.

Heavy use of the building prompted improvements to the dining areas and support spaces. The dining rooms were deemed too small the second year of operation.[89] In fiscal year 1963–64, YPC appropriated, with Superintendent Garrison's approval, $625,000 to install more cafeteria lines, enlarge the dining room and revise the kitchen.

The location—and relocation—of the bar generated a disagreement between NPS and YPC. In YPC's efforts to expand the dining area, it wished to move the bar into the southeast corner of the lounge. Both parties

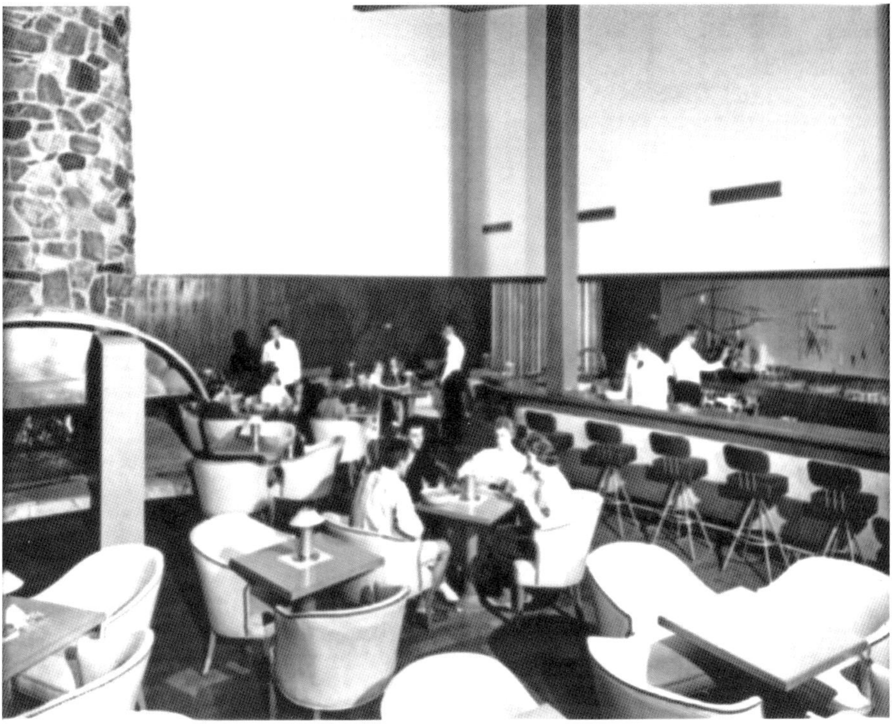

The original bar in Canyon Village Lodge, before its 1964 relocation. *Photo by Rumel, courtesy NPS, YNP, YELL 133489.*

agreed that the lounge was a compensation for "poor caliber of the Village units" and that a portion of the fireplace should be retained for the lounge users. However, on April 27, 1964, NPS suggested that the bar, with a food specialty service, be located in the lower level. YPC noted that this location would be hard to service from the kitchen on the upper level and interpreted on-site verbal communication with NPS on April 25 as approval to relocate the bar to the corner of the lounge and did so. On April 28, YPC submitted NPS with eight copies of the constructed plans, noting that "the length of the bar has been reduced five feet and two inches." YPC's general manager George Beall's twenty-five years in the hotel business guided his relocation decision, driven by his primary interest "to give better service to our guests and, more specifically, to increase the dining space."[90]

Design modifications continued throughout the 1970s and 1980s in response to greater use. The kitchen was extended into what had been the employee's cafeteria at the east end of the kitchen wing and the employee dining room relocated into the lower-level meeting room area (original laundry). In this period, the lounge, gift shop and dining floors were fully carpeted; the star chandeliers painted white; the colorful furniture and line art removed; and restrooms placed between the cafeteria and south dining area. The original ambience and grace of the building eroded incrementally over time.

In 1984 and 2012, the building was upgraded to resist seismic movement. The latter project included reroofing with pre-insulated panels, reinforcing of structural roofing members and incorporation of shear walls at the non-glazed wall areas.

Canyon Administration Building

The Administration Building was originally planned as a two-story building with a manager's office and apartment, accounting, accommodations desk, information counter and fourteen rooms for staff members on the upper level. A lower level was to contain a self-service laundry, public restrooms, nurses' facilities and additional living quarters for employees. This original building was to have a total area of 10,384 square feet. The two-story dormitory extension to the east is visible in the 1955 rendering.

The Administration Building and the Recreation Hall, however, were affected by a $1.5 million error in the original construction estimate. On June 26, 1956 (two days after the groundbreaking), YPC was informed that

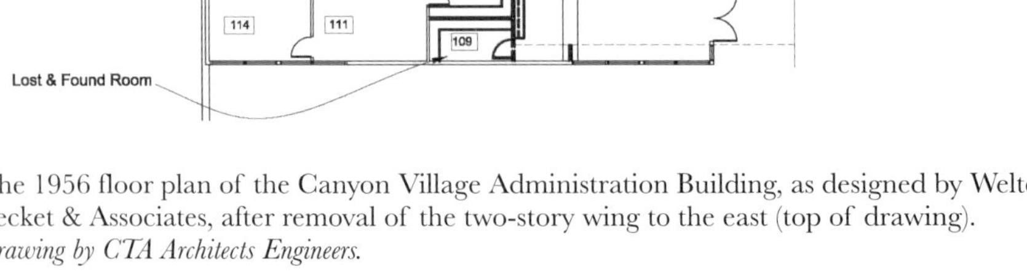

The 1956 floor plan of the Canyon Village Administration Building, as designed by Welton Becket & Associates, after removal of the two-story wing to the east (top of drawing). *Drawing by CTA Architects Engineers.*

the project would cost $4.5 million, based on the working drawings then available. On June 27, YPC held a special board meeting and decided to decrease non-revenue-producing space and increase its loan to $5 million. The board agreed to produce two hundred more hotel units, eliminate the Recreation Hall and reduce the size of the Administration Building.[91]

By July 14, 1956, revised drawings reflected this direction. The Administration Building's dormitory extension was omitted, and the building was reduced to a one-story 2,610-square-foot building with a center space joining two legs of an L-shape. The lobby in the middle was dedicated to registration for the motel cabins. Staff offices, lost-and-found and cabin storage were behind the rental counter; a nurse's office and public restrooms were in the other leg of the "L." The building's orientation and subsidiary relationship to the main lodge, however, remained constant. The roof was low-sloped (yet still gabled) and extended far beyond the building walls. The connective covered walkway to the lodge was retained and sleekly continued into the building as a canopy, directing visitors to the registration desk.

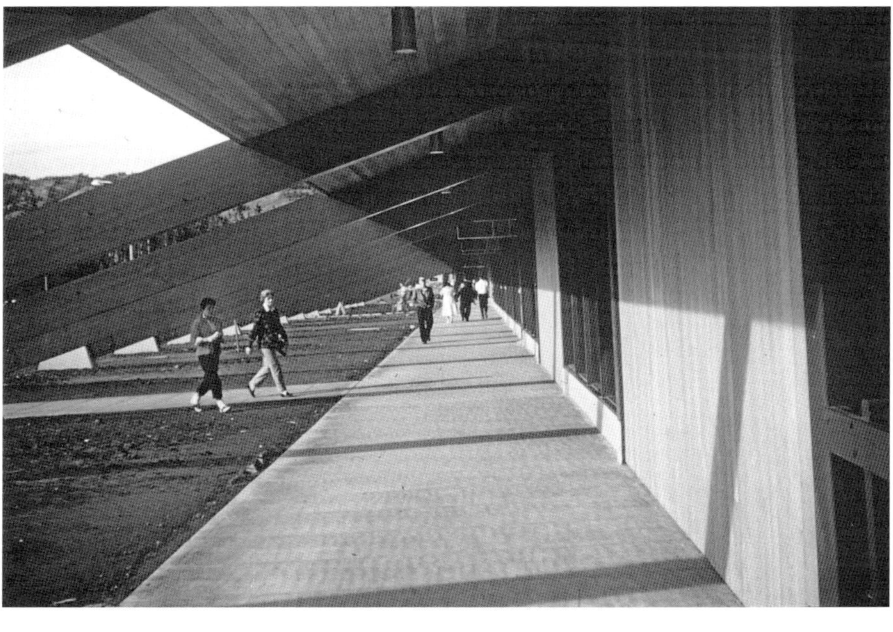

The west walkway at Canyon Village Lodge directed visitors north to the Administration Building, 1957. *Photo by Haynes Studios Inc., courtesy of MHS RCPA Haynes Foundation Collection.*

As with the lodge, the companion Administration Building has glazing set in wood mullions above a concrete base and clerestories to let in more light—particularly above the solid wall planes finished with natural finished wood. A stone wall at the north side is a planar component that slides past the office glazing. The space between the Administration Building and the lodge is a generous patio allowing for indecision and lingering.

Canyon Recreation Hall (Unbuilt)

Design of the Recreation Hall was concurrent with that of the lodge and Administration Building—the three formed a unit to be connected with covered walkways. This composition was shown in the first renderings, which also showed the strong visual similarity of the hall to the lodge. The Recreation Hall was a smaller version of the lodge, with similar rectangular footprint, a long side-gabled roof and glu-lam beams extending to the ground. The hall was to continue the established tradition of entertainment that had been provided in the old Canyon Lodge lobby, which had a long-practiced culture of staff ("savages") entertaining the visitors ("dudes") that had become a highlight of the tourist package. The modern version was to be adaptable for various uses such as dances, movies and stage productions by staff. With a total area of 16,500 square feet, it would have a capacity for one thousand movable seats.[92]

WB&A's 1955 renderings show the Recreation Hall west of the lodge. The length of the hall was oriented east–west, with the entry on the north side facing the parking lot. Grade dropped at the south side to the lower level of the site. One rendering provoked specific comment from Frank Mattson, in his official capacity as YNP's landscape architect: "Those of us who have worked in parks for some period may become obsessed with the idea we wish to see structures subordinated to the terrain. Therefore, a building which does appear more or less completely stable has greater appeal than one which does not. Do others also see the broken back and the poise for flight which has already been expressed?"[93]

The sweeping and soaring roof of the proposed Recreation Hall was perhaps proposed too early for NPS to appreciate, but it might have helped set the stage for future attempts at more dynamic and expressive designs. Subsequent Mission 66 buildings—such as the Saint Mary Visitor Center, constructed in Glacier National Park between 1964 and

1966—had upsweeping roofs that paid homage to the steep and ragged mountains in the background.

WB&A provided a more modest roof design, a smaller and shorter version of the lodge roof, in a subsequent rendering. The cross-section of the building was most likely similar also, as interior stairs connected the main level to a lower one, to the south. The drawings show that the tall gable roof shape was to be exposed on the interior, interrupted by a closed mezzanine like that in the lodge. The ceiling was to be finished with an acoustical tile ceiling in accordance with the building function. A long snack bar extended across the width of the building, adjacent to a ticket booth by the outside wall. The interior was to be fitted with a large auditorium space, a projection room, dressing rooms and restrooms.[94]

At the June 24, 1956 groundbreaking for Canyon Village, the Recreation Hall was still included in the project. Construction was delayed two days afterward in response to the revised cost estimate. In March 1957, the YPC board considered having the building's foundation poured to take advantage of McNeil's presence (and equipment) on site. The $40,000 cost proved too much to take on. YPC decided to continue hosting entertainment in the Canyon Hotel lobby until the Recreation Hall could be built.

After Canyon Hotel was closed in 1959, the meeting rooms in the lower level of Canyon Village Lodge were used for recreation—movies, dancing and ping-pong, as well as Sunday church services. It was still hoped in 1965 that the Recreation Hall would be built, as it was "intended to house the recreational functions eventually. The building also will provide meeting space for large groups."[95] The assigned site remains open today.

Hamilton's Store and Dormitory

The development's cohesive appearance was due to the site layout, as well as WB&A's role in designing Hamilton's new general store and dormitory building. Hamilton's store and Haynes's photo shops were an integral part of every Park site and were included in the Canyon-area studies and master plans from the 1930s and 1950s. The Park's master plan from March 1952 estimated a cost of $350,000 for the general store and associated dormitory.[96] Hamilton typically used local architects and seems to have had plans drawn up for this store at another site at the time he finally engaged WB&A in February 1956. In his January 1956 conversation with Jack Beardwood at WB&A, he referred to existing plans that he would pay WB&A a flat fee to revise, to fit the new site.[97] Beardwood's feeling that WB&A would not receive this commission was unwarranted, for it did receive the project and provide a design that incorporated many of the same features used on the lodge. The Park's Frank Mattson was pleased at the commission, feeling it would harmonize the store's design with the other buildings.

The dormitory was identical to those built for YPC, and the store was similar in appearance to the lodge. WB&A was able to apply many of the same details—in fact, the same drawing sheets (labeled for "All Buildings")—for the store. The massing was simpler than the lodge's, yet the systems, materials and treatment were comparable. The store was also built into the hillside, with the main level at grade with the parking lot and the two-story portion facing the rear service area. The store's T-shaped footprint mimicked the lodge's: the main retail space was two hundred feet long by sixty feet wide, and the center intersecting wing was sixty feet wide by eighty feet long. The same roofing details (and wood shake finish) were incorporated into the cross gables of low-sloped roofs (3.5:12), with same-height ridges capped with copper. The walls were configured in the established twenty-foot bays between the wood glu-lam columns, with a storefront of reduced glass area set above plywood panels. The end walls were a direct reflection of the end walls of the lodge, with diagonal wood boards set into full-height panels aligned with the extended ridge beams. The tongue-and-groove ceiling boards spanned between the exposed glu-lam beams that supported the sloped roofs. These similarities enabled WB&A to complete the final design and drawings by June 8, 1956.

The construction cost of $512,000—and probably the twelve-thousand-square-foot area—were greater than the 1952 estimate. The dormitory cost $225,000 to build.

An earlier document was reviewed by YNP during the March 10, 1956 Gardiner full-team design conference. Mattson's meeting summary included a comment that the Hamilton dorm would be an obstruction to the foot traffic from cabin Loop A and that the dorm should be with the YPC dorms, where it would also be closer to the employee cafeteria in the lodge.[98] The dorm was not placed with the others but was perhaps located closer to the store.

The store's design attracted as much attention as the lodge's. The soda fountain was a large draw and was reported to be "conspicuous in its modernistic design, luminiferous overall ceiling and a seating capacity of

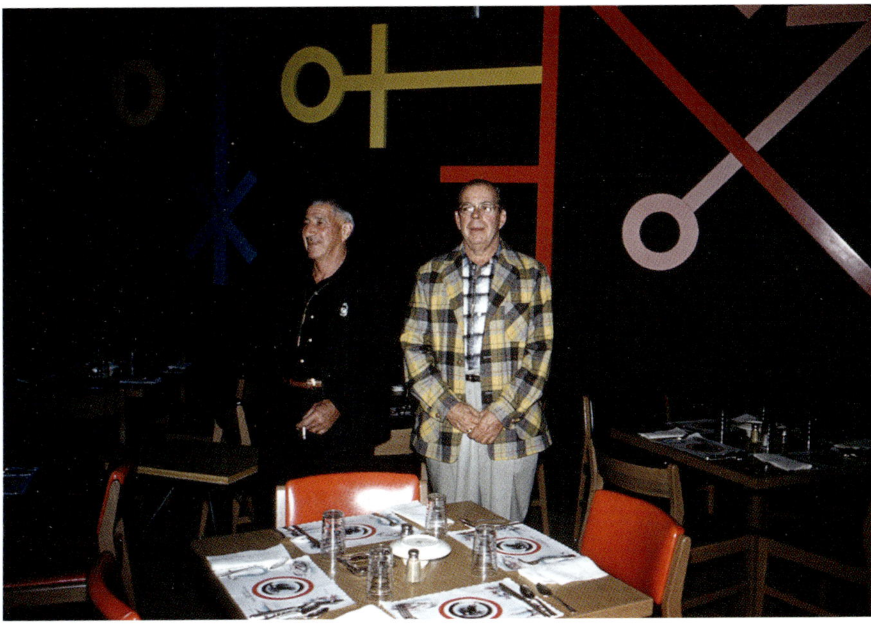

The colorful line art in the Canyon Village Lodge Dining Room showed up against the dark background, 1957. *Courtesy of George and Kathryn Bornemann Yellowstone Collection.*

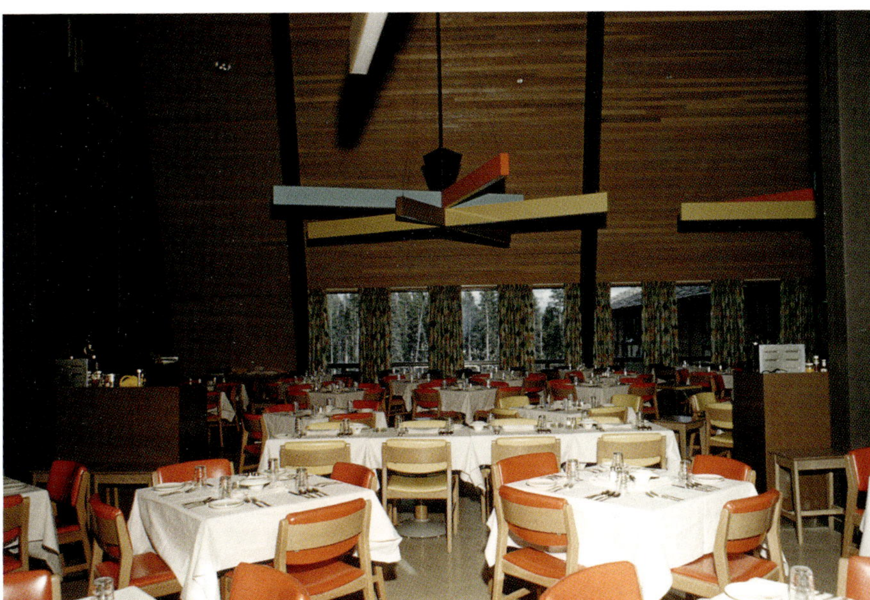

The dining room furnishings and drapes were selected and procured by Stone & Glass Ltd., 1957. *Photo by Haynes Studios Inc., courtesy of MHS RCPA Haynes Foundation Collection.*

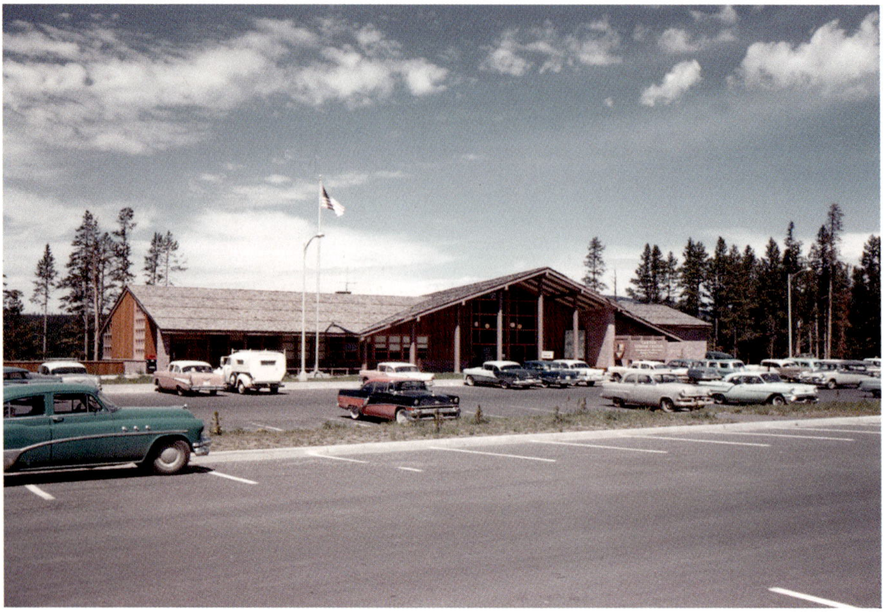

Hurt and Trudell's design of the Canyon Visitor Center responded to the Park Service's needs at the time of construction, 1957. *Courtesy of George and Kathryn Bornemann Yellowstone Collection.*

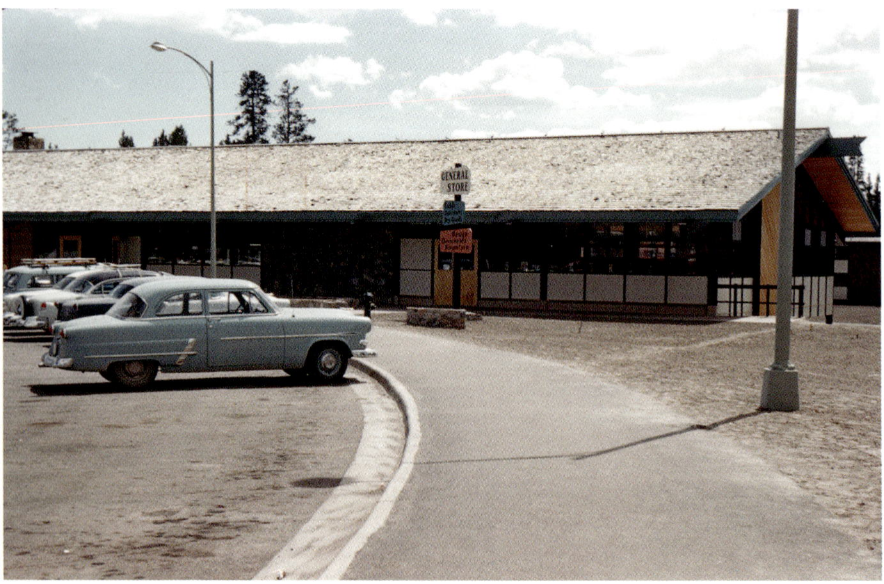

Hamilton's Store massing was similar to Canyon Village Lodge's, yet the expression of the glu-lam beams was greatly reduced; the glu-lams did not extend out to grade. Note the compatibility of colors between the building and signage and the cars, 1957. *Courtesy of George and Kathryn Bornemann Yellowstone Collection.*

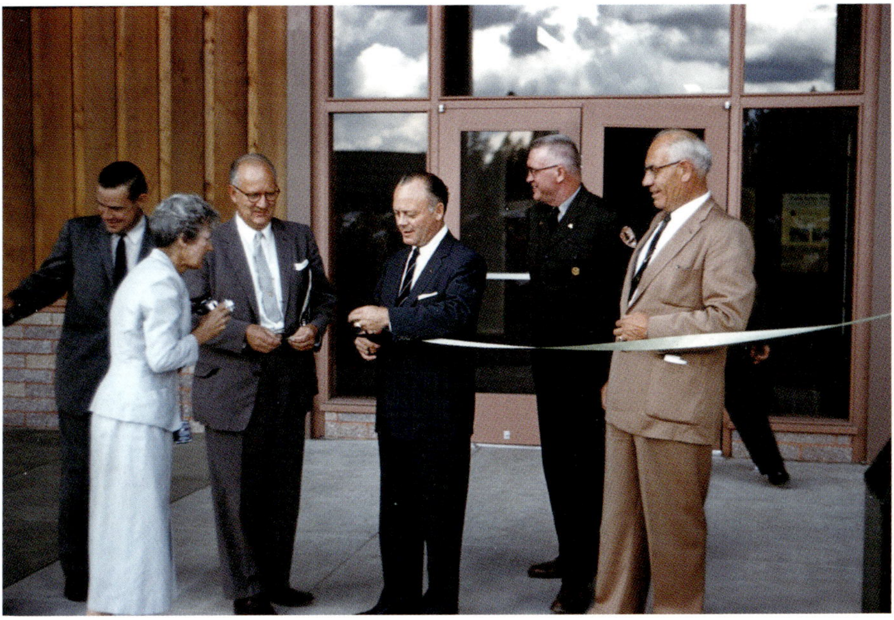

August 17, 1958 dedication ceremony at Canyon Village Visitor Center. Wirth (*third from left*) is sporting the light-color tie. *Courtesy of George and Kathryn Bornemann Yellowstone Collection.*

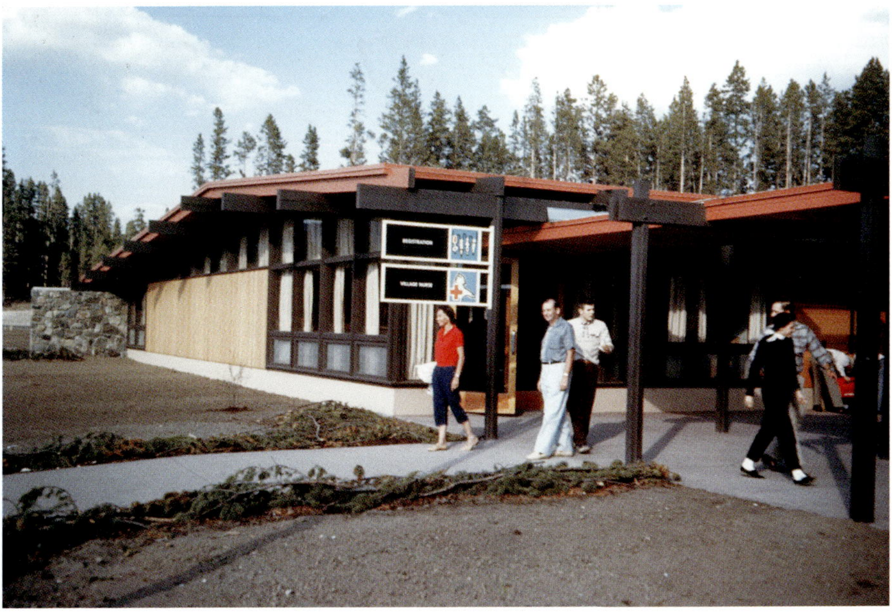

The covered walkway provided a strong connection between Canyon Village Lodge and the Administration Building, shown at left, 1957. *Photo by Jack Ellis Haynes of Haynes Studios Inc., courtesy of MHS RCPA Haynes Foundation Collection.*

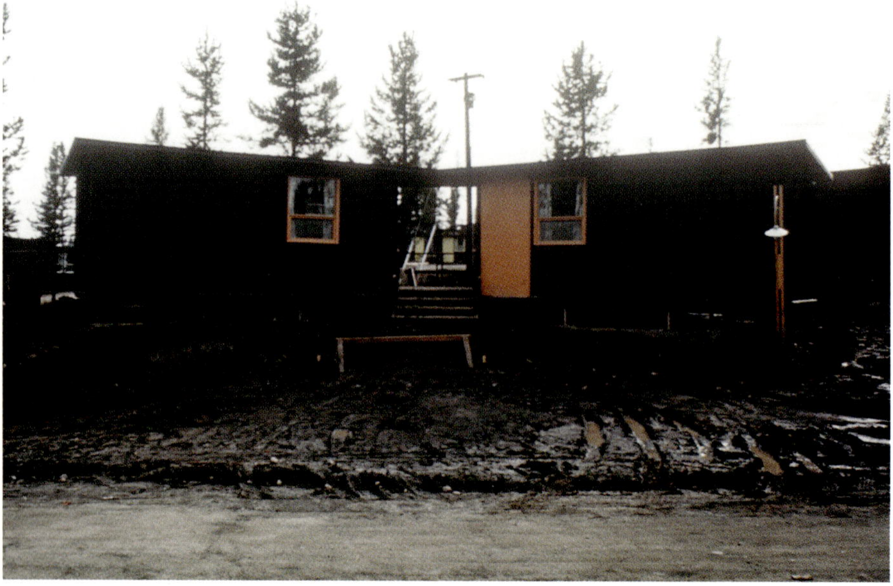

Cabin Type C (Frontier Cabins) had three-sided wings joined with open passageways at the hinge point, 1957. *Photo by Haynes Studios Inc., courtesy of MHS RCPA Haynes Foundation Collection.*

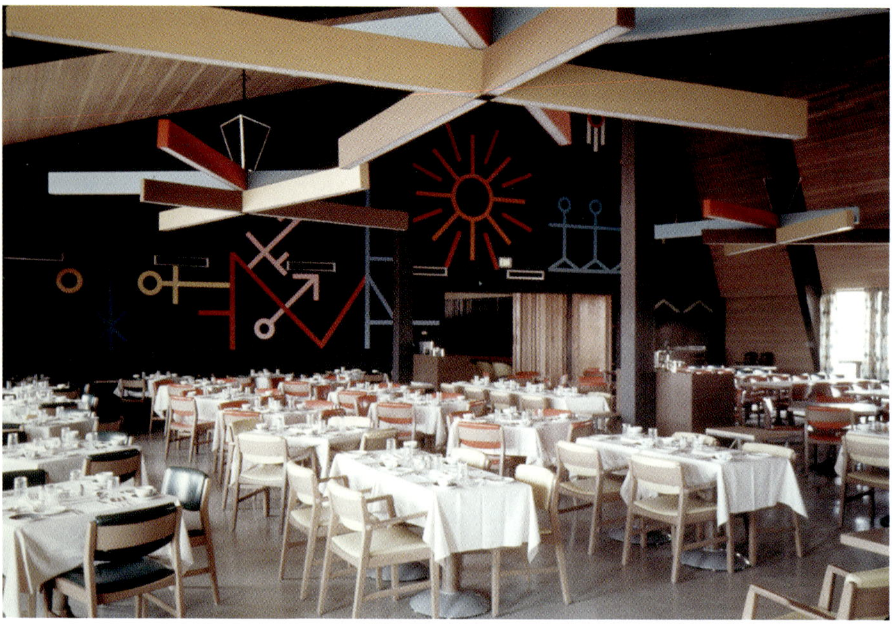

Canyon Village Lodge's dining room was full of color—in the upholstery, light fixtures and the line art on the north wall, 1957. *Photo by Haynes Studios Inc., courtesy of MHS RCPA Haynes Foundation Collection.*

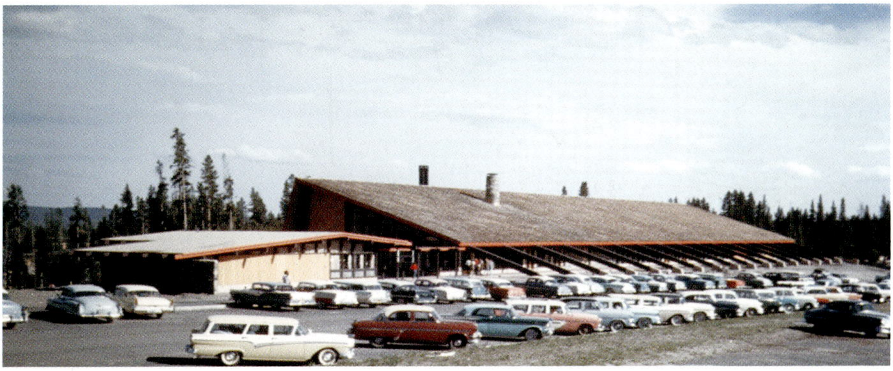

Canyon Village Lodge and Administration Building from northwest, 1957. *Photo by Jack Ellis Haynes of Haynes Studios Inc., courtesy of MHS RCPA Haynes Foundation Collection.*

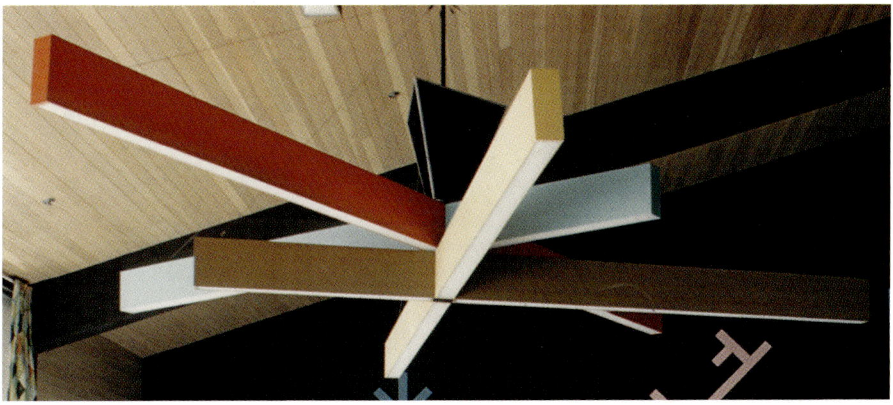

The starlight chandeliers in Canyon Village Lodge provided a consistent and welcome plane of varying colors above head height, 1957. *Photo by Haynes Studios Inc., courtesy of MHS RCPA Haynes Foundation Collection.*

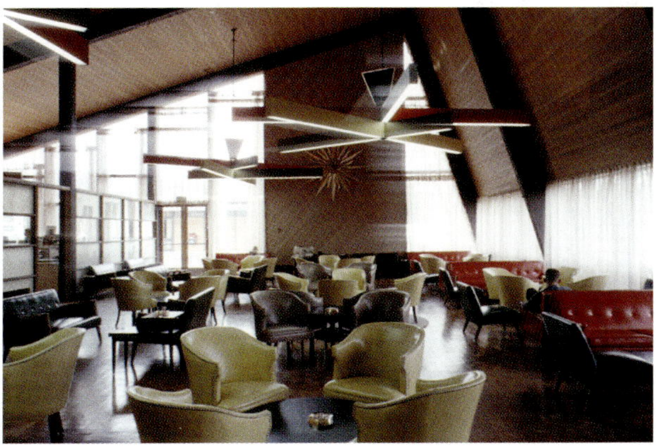

The sunburst clock at the north wall of the Canyon Village Lodge lounge reinforced the end wall's expression as an overmantel, 1957. *Photo by Haynes Studios Inc., courtesy of MHS RCPA Haynes Foundation Collection.*

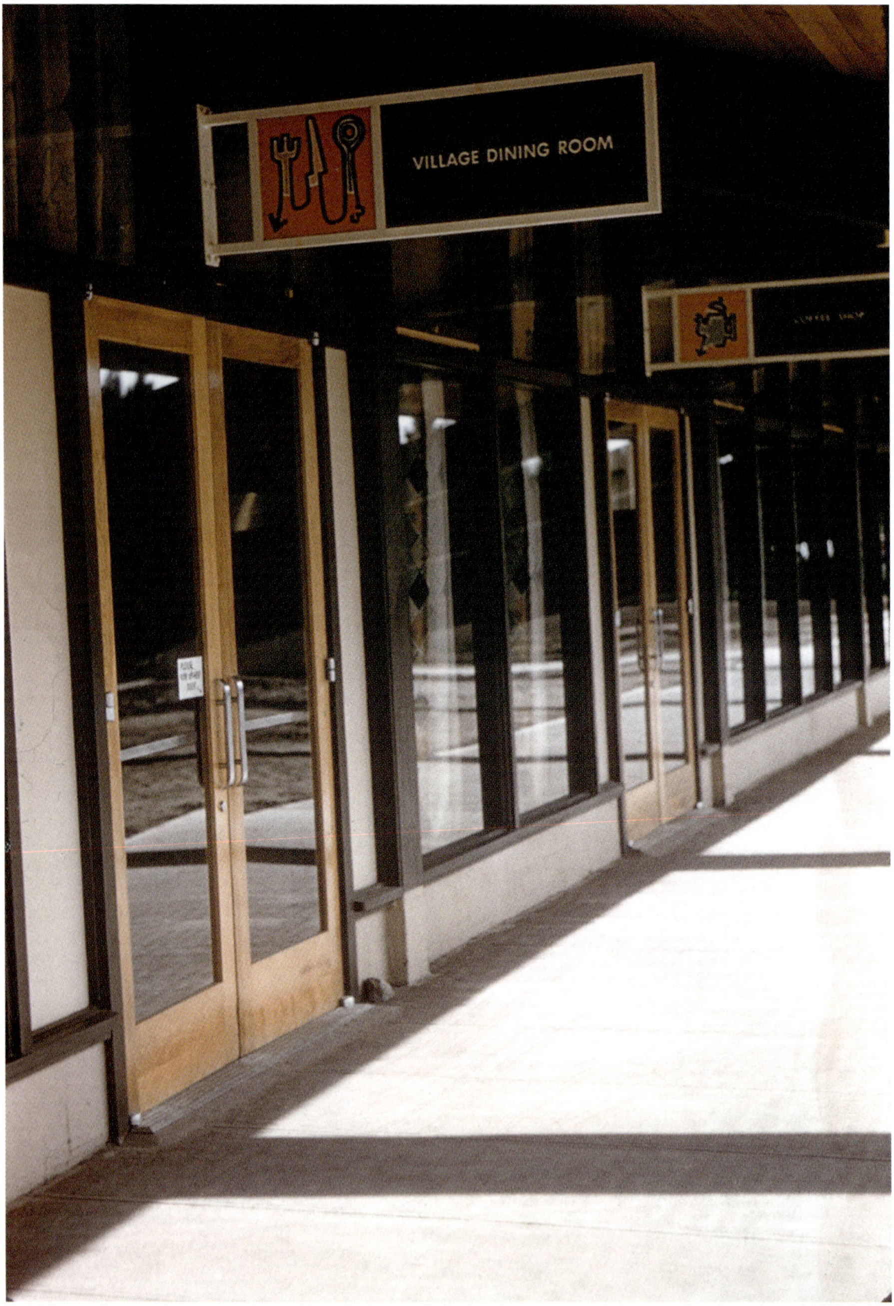

The blade signs that announced the various functions within Canyon Village Lodge were colorful and playful, 1957. *Photo by Haynes Studios Inc., courtesy of MHS RCPA Haynes Foundation Collection.*

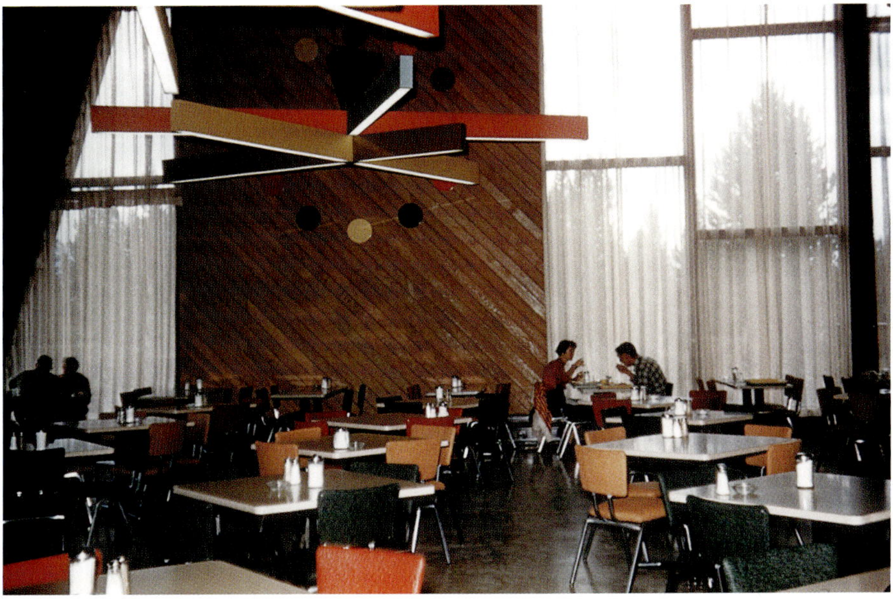

The George Nelson–style clock at the south wall of the Canyon Village Lodge cafeteria was about ten feet in diameter, 1957. *Photo by Haynes Studios Inc., courtesy of MHS RCPA Haynes Foundation Collection.*

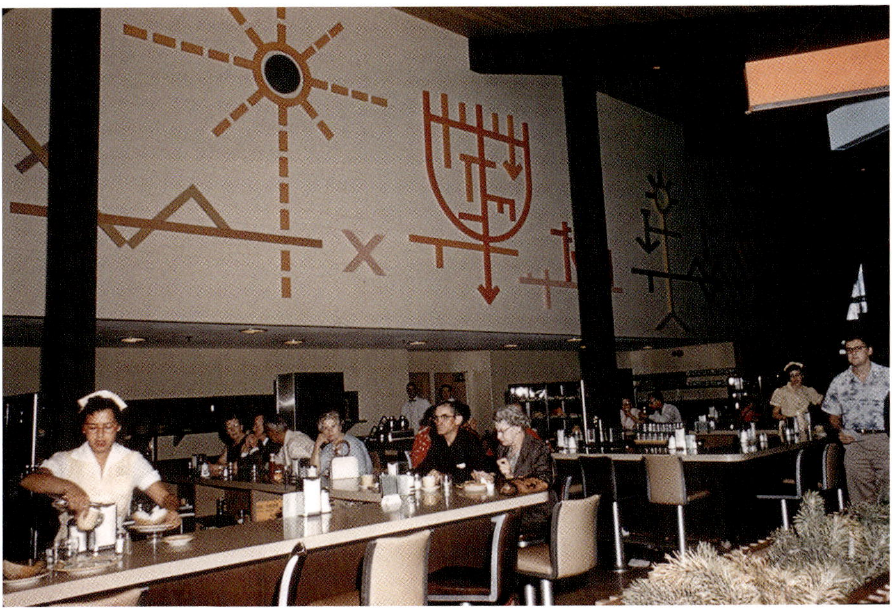

The line art on the front of the mezzanine above the Canyon Village Lodge coffee shop was striking due its scale and sparseness, 1957. *Photo by Haynes Studios Inc., courtesy of MHS RCPA Haynes Foundation Collection.*

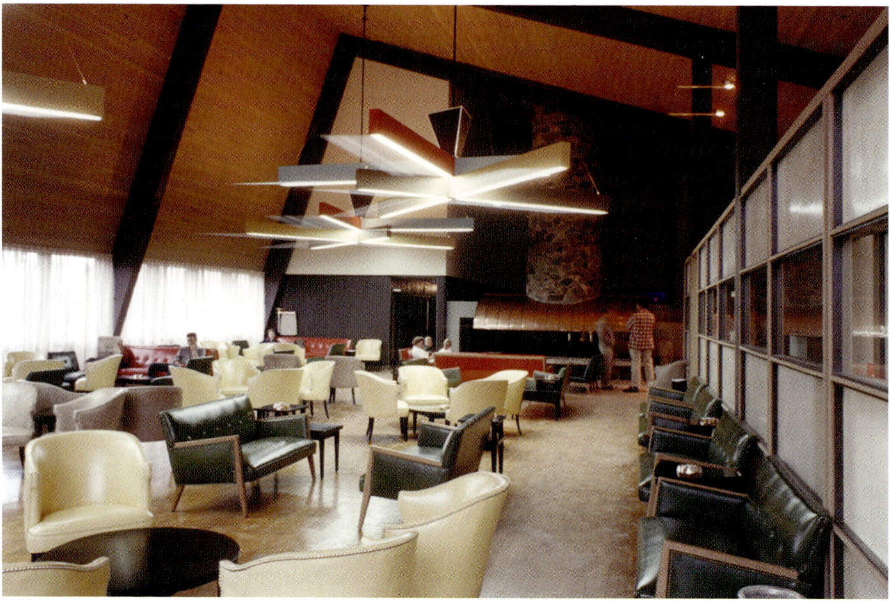

The Canyon Village Lodge lounge, looking south toward the fireplace, 1957. The translucent walls of the gift shop are visible at right. This interior was well received upon opening. *Photo by Haynes Studios Inc., courtesy of MHS RCPA Haynes Foundation Collection.*

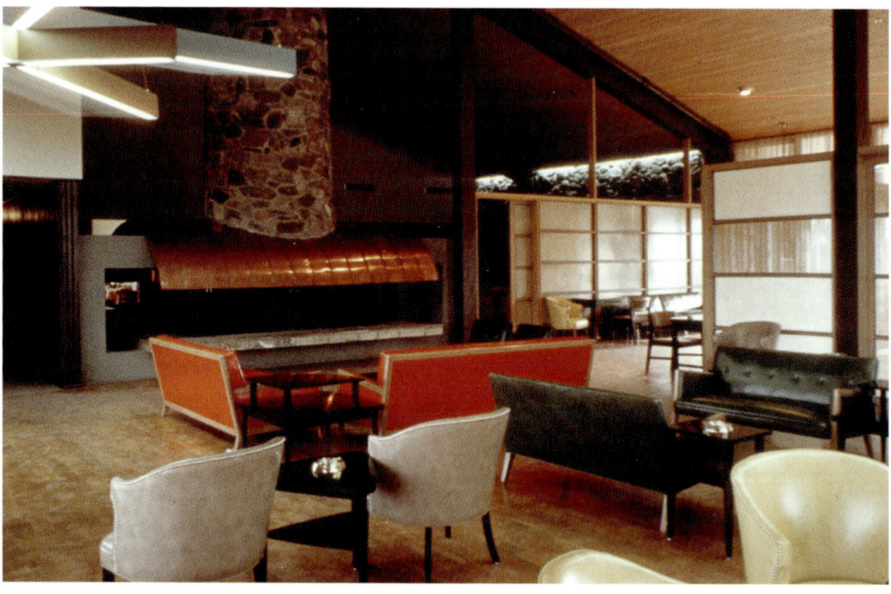

The neutral-colored walls and lone row of columns provided a contrasting background to the colorful furniture, the screen walls and the expressive texture of the stone chimney above the gleaming copper of the seamed fireplace hood, 1957. *Photo by Haynes Studios Inc., courtesy of MHS RCPA Haynes Foundation Collection.*

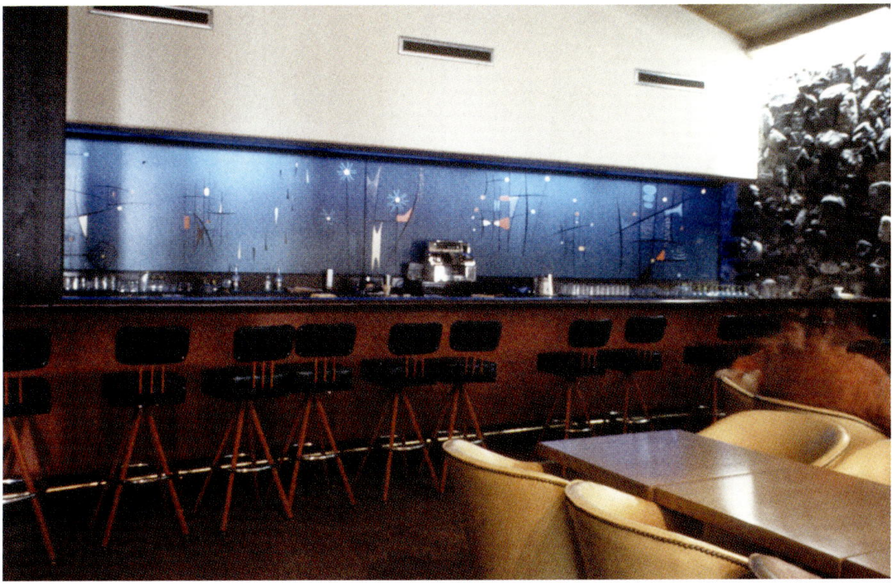

The elegant bar east of the Canyon Village Lodge lounge was an artful composition with Miró-like illuminated back bar, 1957. *Photo by Haynes Studios Inc., courtesy of MHS RCPA Haynes Foundation Collection.*

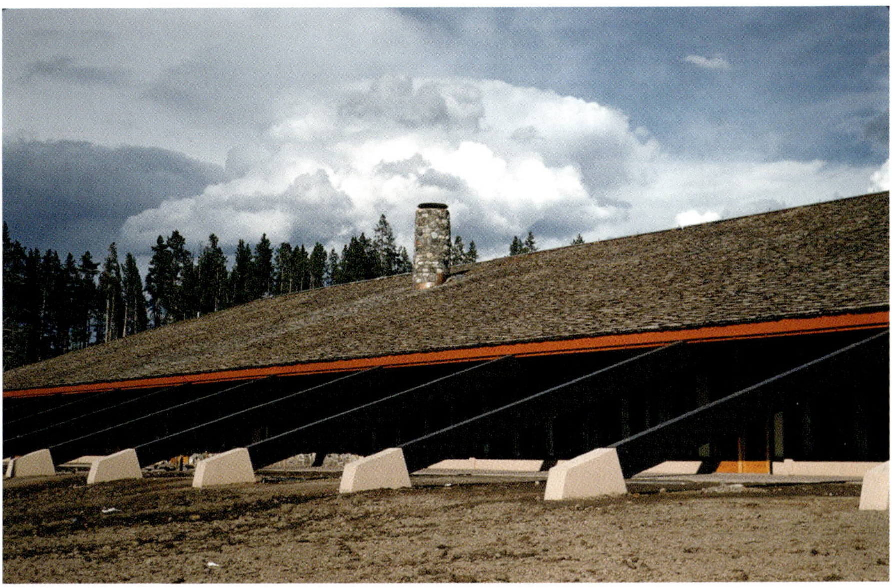

Canyon Village Lodge was imbued with simplicity and clarity. The structural strength of the long glu-lam beams and the broad plane of the roof informed visitors of the expansive space within, 1957. *Photo by Haynes Studios Inc., courtesy of MHS RCPA Haynes Foundation Collection.*

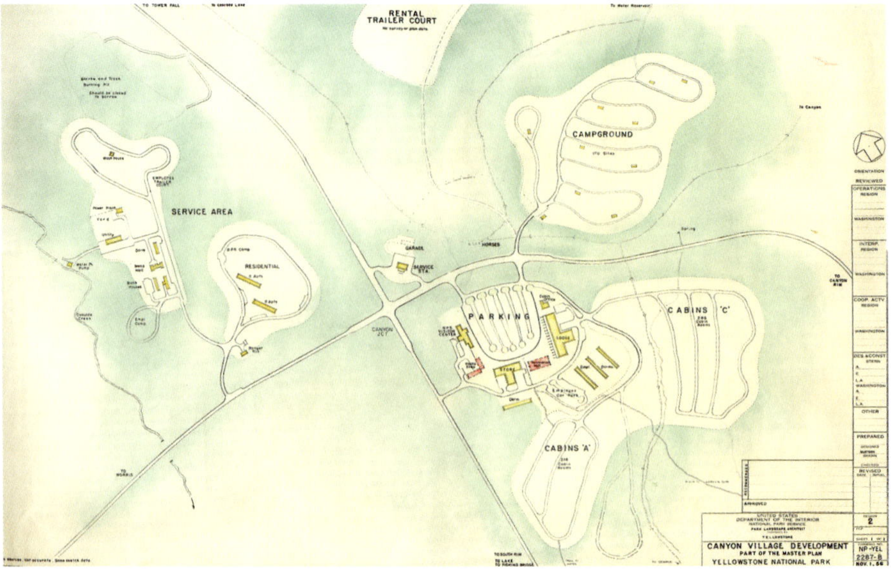

Canyon Village Development, map prepared by Frank Mattson, 1956. *Courtesy NPS, YNP.*

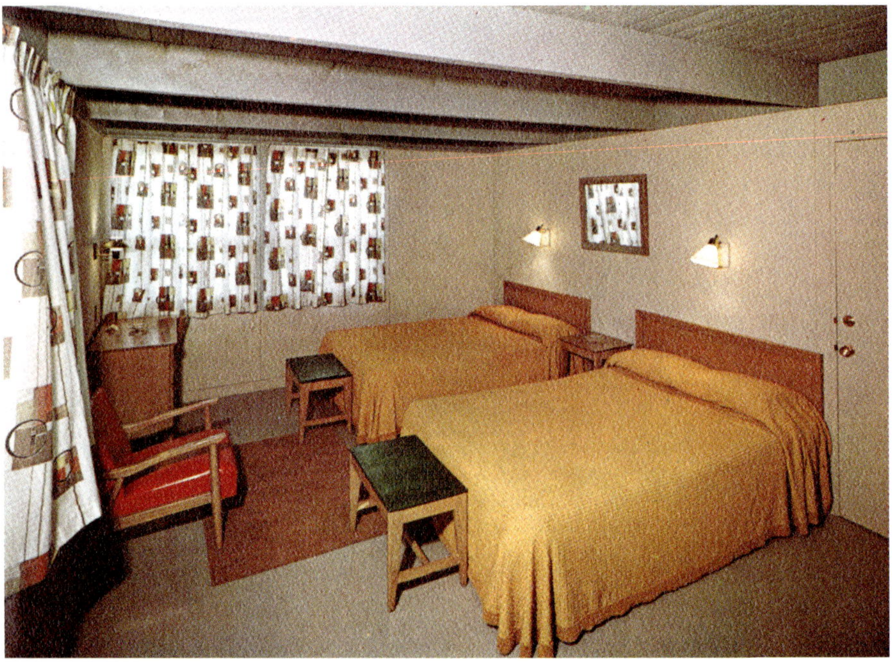

The Yellowstone Park Company promoted the new Canyon Village cabins in its colorful brochure from 1957. *YPC photo, courtesy NPS, YNP, YELL 127179-1.*

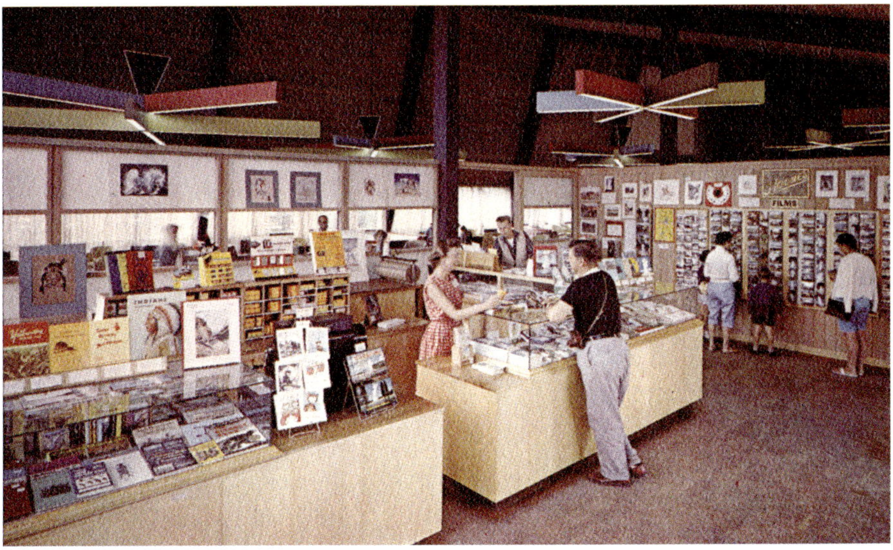

Temporary Haynes Photo Shop in the Canyon Village Lodge Gift Shop, looking southeast, circa 1957. Haynes was in the lodge until the shop was completed in 1960. *Courtesy NPS, YNP, YELL 127179-2.*

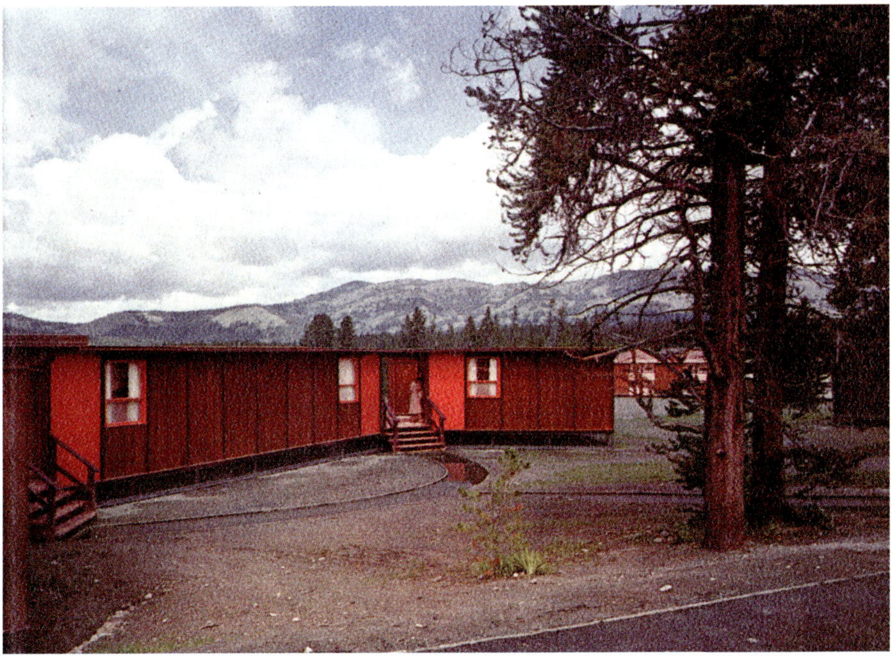

The cabin doors were color-coded for ease of identification, circa 1957. *YPC photo, courtesy of NPS, YNP, YELL 127179-3.*

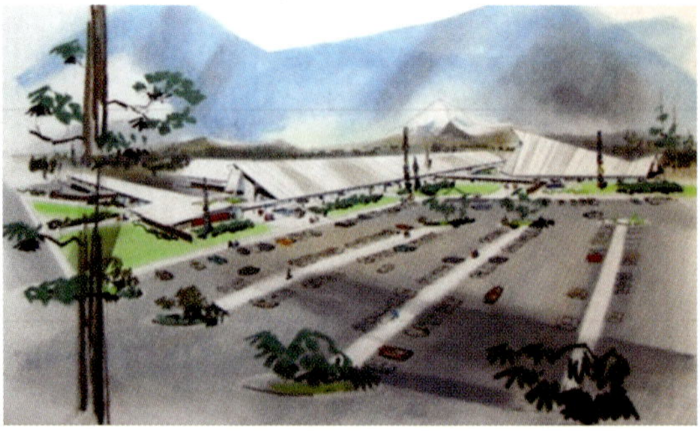

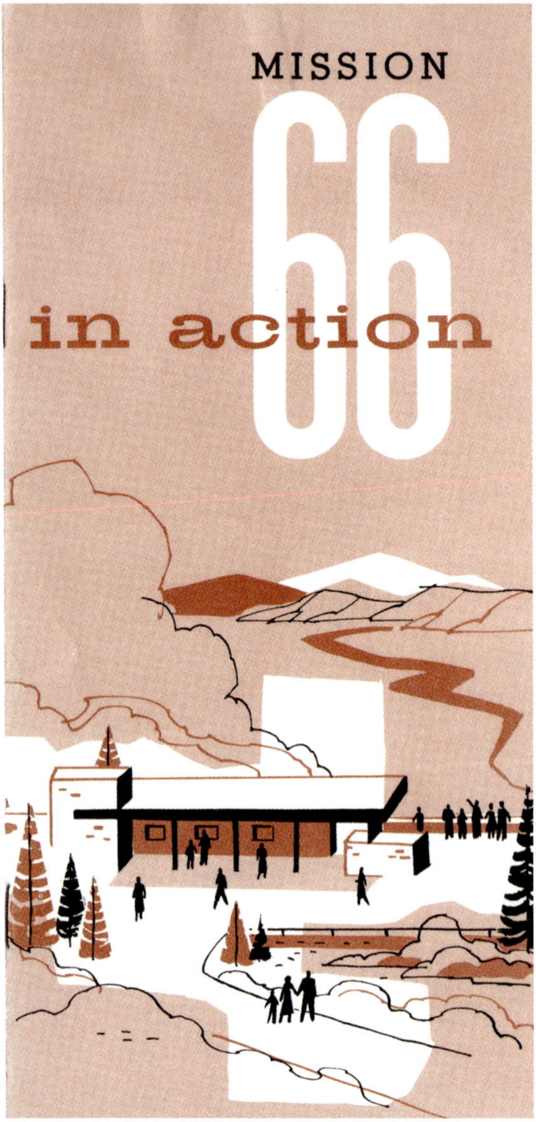

Top: The dynamic sweeping roofs of the Recreation Hall (building at right), as rendered by Welton Becket & Associates in 1955, were seen as a "broken back" by YNP's landscape architect Frank Mattson. *Render courtesy of AECOM.*

Left: The 1961 NPS Mission 66 brochure, with promotional descriptions of the program similar to those in the earlier versions of this publication. *Courtesy NPS, YNP, Coll. 185385 YELL 185385-67.*

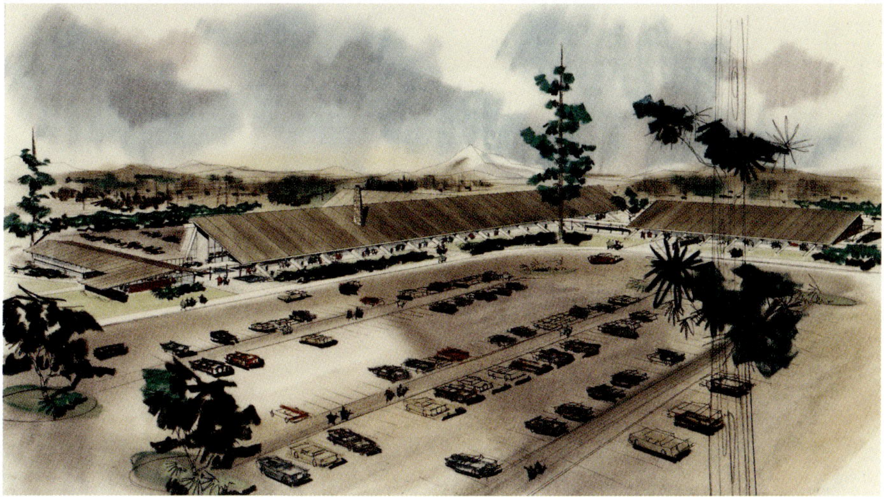

October 1955 Welton Becket & Associates' rendering of Canyon Village, looking southeast, with Canyon Lodge in the center, flanked by the Administration Building at the left and the Recreation Hall on the right. The large roof expanses were rendered as brown sheet metal, and a reflecting pool was depicted at the north (*left*) end of the lodge. *Render courtesy of AECOM.*

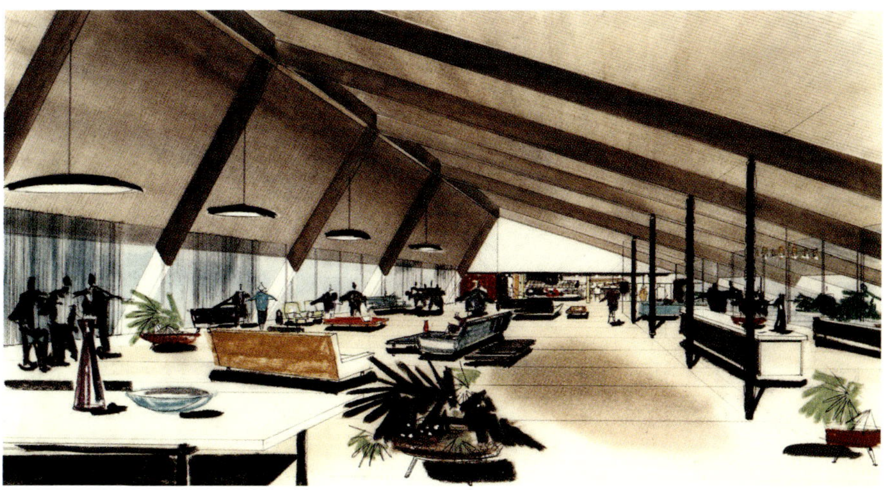

Welton Becket & Associates' October 1955 rendering of Canyon Village Lounge, looking south, depicting a grand, open volume unlike any in the Park before. The ceiling structure reflects the steep roofs that Mattson remarked on. *Render courtesy of AECOM.*

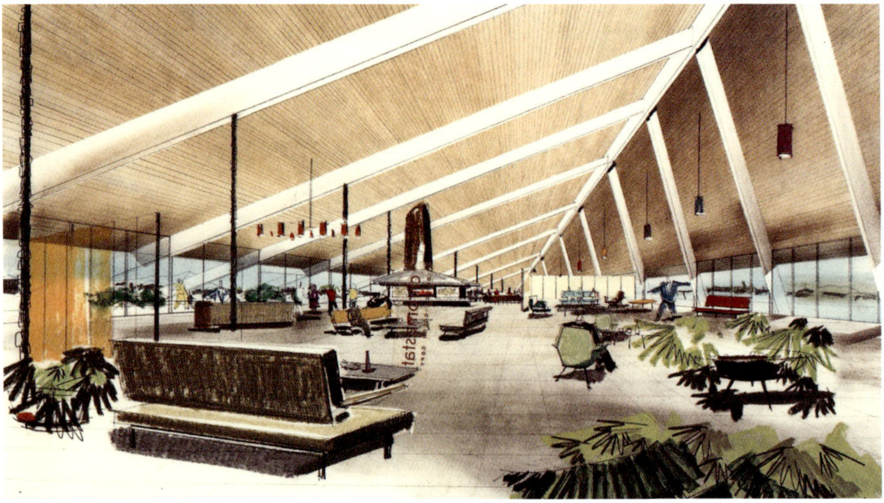

Welton Becket & Associates' October 1955 colored rendering of the Canyon Village Lodge lounge, looking north toward the fireplace, showed the huge expanse of unfettered volume enhanced by full-height glazing at the lower side walls. *Render courtesy of AECOM.*

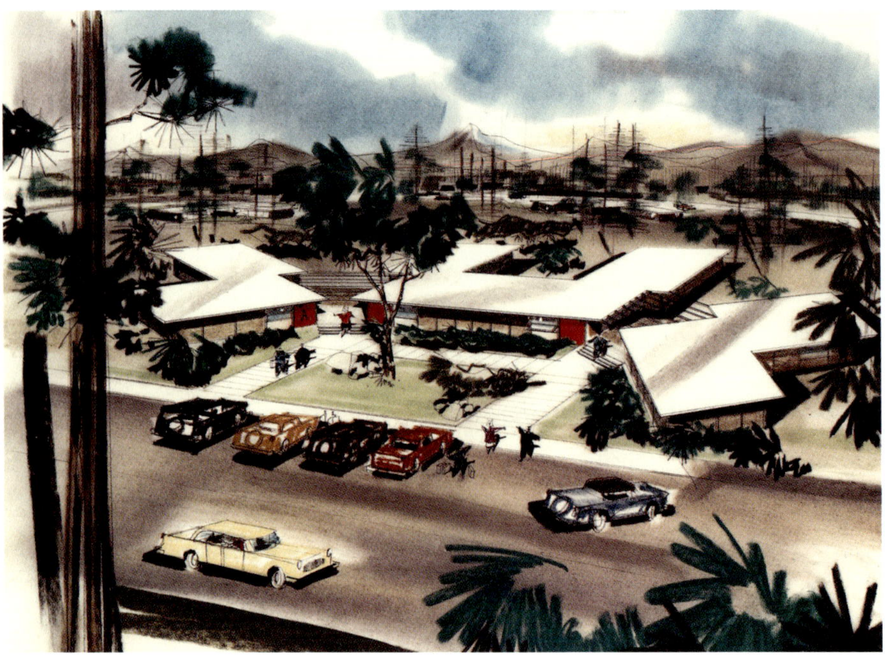

Welton Becket & Associates' 1955 colored rendering of the cabins reflects the goal of stimulating communal experience among the happy visitors. *Render courtesy of AECOM.*

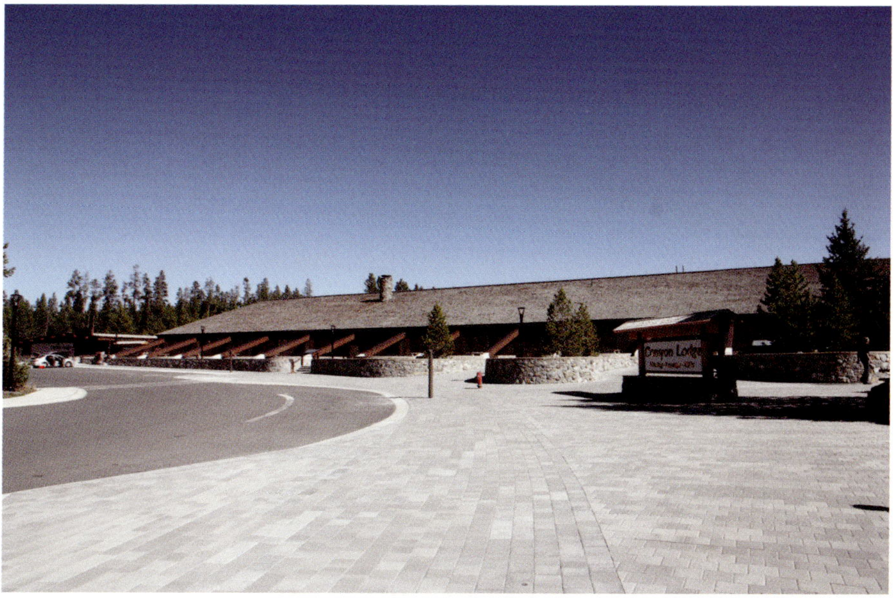

Canyon Village Lodge exterior in 2015, with softened landscaping walls and prevalent dark-brown trim. *Photo by the author.*

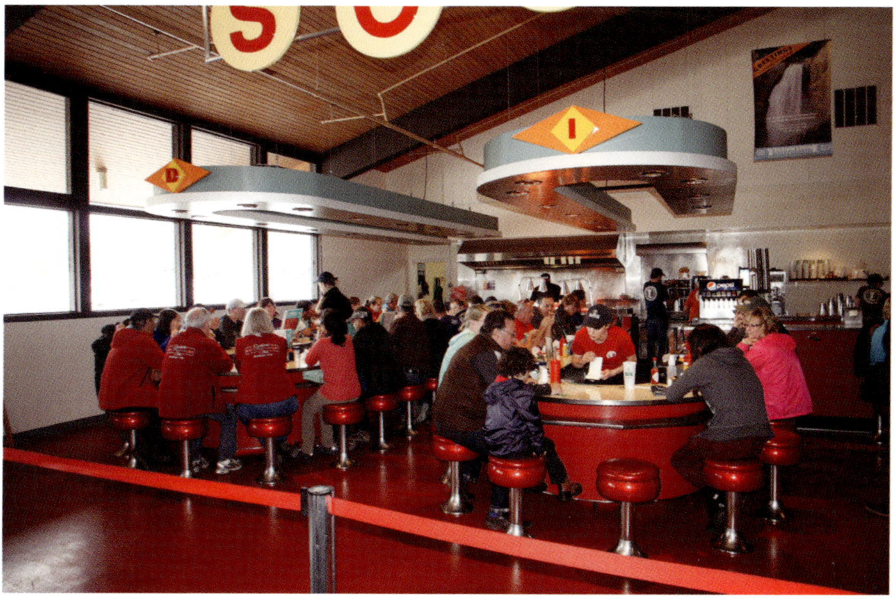

Canyon Village Hamilton General Store, with newly remodeled soda foundation, 2015.

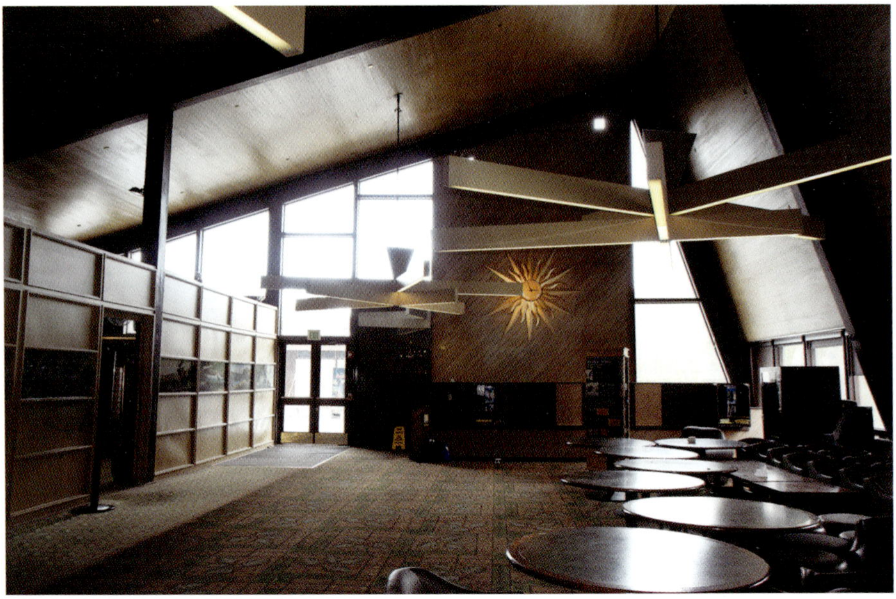

Canyon Village Lodge Lounge in 2015, looking north. *Photo by the author.*

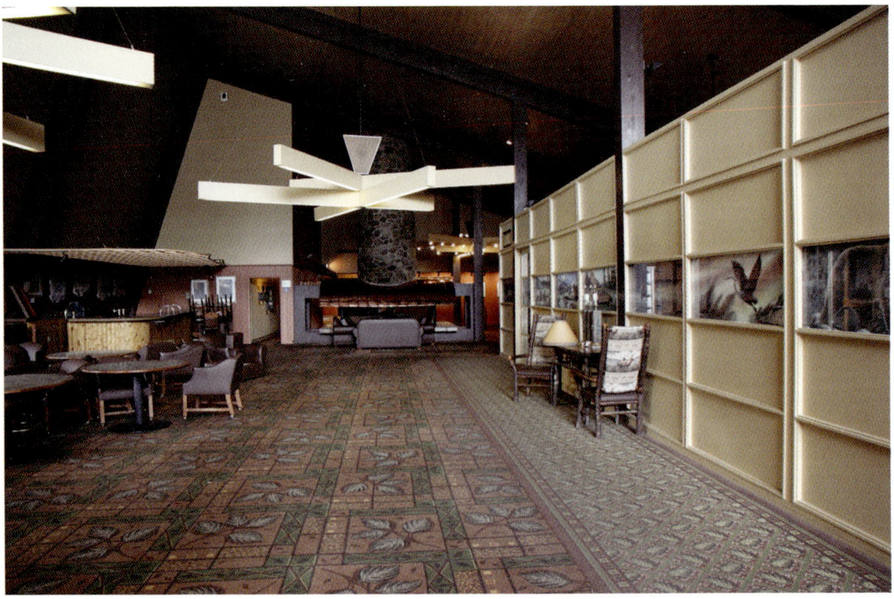

In the 1980s, the interior walls of the Canyon Village Lodge Gift Shop were increased in height and fitted with opaque panels. Photo looking south in the lounge, 2016. *Photo by the author.*

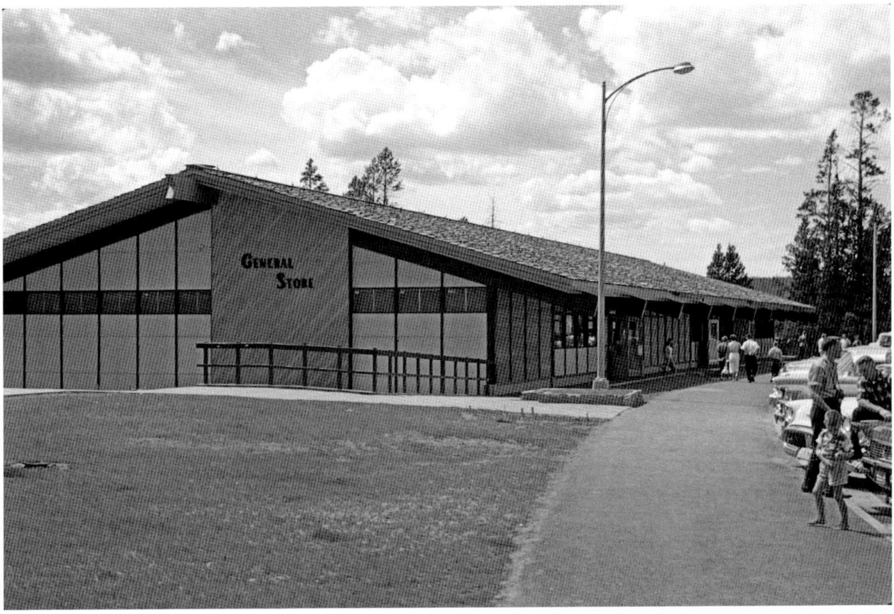

Welton Becket & Associates' design for Hamilton's General Store utilized the architectural vocabulary already established at Canyon Village Lodge, 1957. *Courtesy of George and Kathryn Bornemann Yellowstone Collection.*

100."[99] Despite the fast pace of the design and construction, the walls were decorated with "murals—One 12' x 60' depicting animal life in Yellowstone Park, Yellowstone Falls, and scenic beauty of various points of interest."[100] (The murals are no longer extant.) Similar reviews were stated in local newspaper and Canyon Village newsletter accounts.

HAYNES PHOTO SHOP

The Haynes Photo Shop design was developed later than the WB&A designs. In the meantime, Haynes shared space with the gift shop in the northwest corner of the new lodge. Bozeman architect William E. Grabow submitted the working drawings for NPS review in June 1958. The final drawings were ready for bid in January 1959, with a tentative bid due date of February 20, 1959.[101]

Grabow's design was of the prevalent modernist theme and incorporated some of the same materials used in the other buildings. The relationship to the raised site was similar as well; the rear wing of this L-shaped building was two-story. The main portion of the building that fronted the parking lot was the single-level store. A low-sloped (1.5:12) front-gable roof extended over the full-height storefront glazing, providing transparency at the retail level. Glu-lam beams spanned from interior support to the exterior, with additional beams supporting trellises at the entry. The established grid within the structure produced a regular alternating pattern on the side walls of vertical wood siding and glazing.

Two noticeable deviations from the WB&A-designed buildings was the use of built-up roofing and of split-face concrete block at the base of the storefront. The stacked bond of long, thin block had become a signature of the period; this was used (to NPS's dismay) at the visitor center as well.

Given the timing, Jack Haynes had the proposed design reviewed by the participants of the NPS Park Development Conference held at Canyon Village in September 1957. The team recommended that "the sign shown in the architect's drawing be eliminated or made to conform with the uniform sign pattern followed throughout Canyon Village."[102] The proposed sign was a vertical plane composed of seven vertical posts higher than the building's

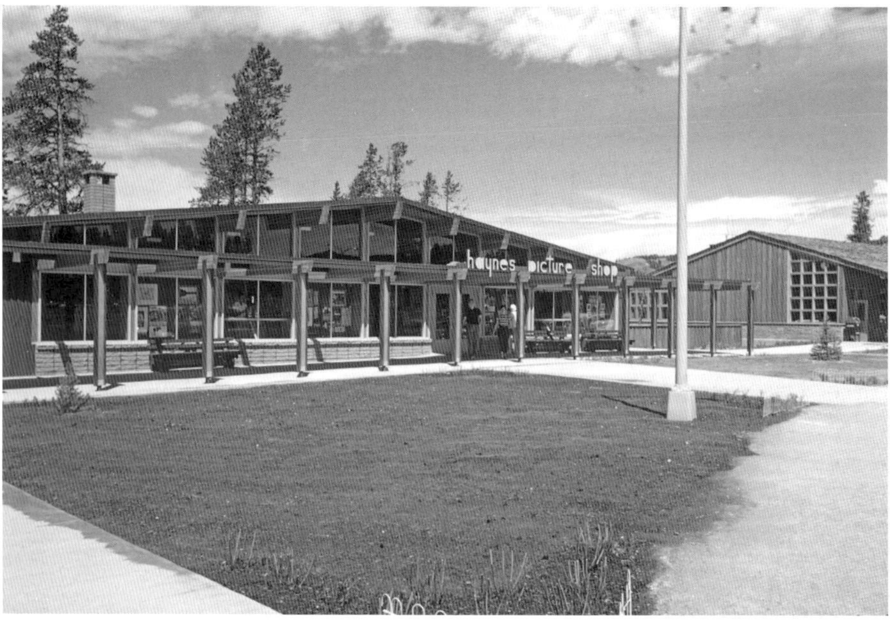

William Grabow's design for the Haynes Photo Shop building incorporated similar design components and materials used elsewhere in Canyon Village, 1957. *Courtesy of George and Kathryn Bornemann Yellowstone Collection.*

ridge, spaced to fit letter panels (conveniently six, "Haynes," over six, "Studio") between them. Placed in front of the building, its movie theater style was objectionable, thus it was not constructed. The sign ultimately used was of white rounded block letters set on the entry pergola.

CANYON VISITOR CENTER

The visitor center was the one building within the commercial area constructed for NPS and designed to fit the new building type that would help tourists interpret the Grand Canyon resource. NPS director Wirth provided some guidance to accompany this new typology in a memo he issued to all field offices in February 1956: "[G]enerally speaking, we will use the term Visitor Center in place of the terms museum-administration building, public use building, and in some cases, in place of Park Headquarters when it is a point of visitor concentration. However, there will be many cases where it will be necessary to designate both a park headquarters building and a visitor center." This statement was intended to promote proper usage of the terms in printed matter—text and maps.[103]

There continued to be confusion in the field regarding the role and operation of the visitor center, which the Mission 66 Advisory Committee tried to clear up in September 1957. The committee recommended that the centers should serve multiple functions and be designed for future expansion. It also advised that each park should develop its own program to meet its needs—primarily as to whether the center would provide interpretation or direct the visitors to interpretive sites. Either way, the building should be the most dominant building in the development.[104]

Given that the visitor center was a new building type for the parks, these directions were not a guarantee that the selected functions would serve well over time. At Canyon, specific requests were made that related to prior experience; it had been difficult to envision the new concept. For instance, early design drawings by architects Hurt & Trudell of San Francisco generated comments in January 1955 from YNP's chief ranger, Otto M. Brown, to the acting superintendent. He asked for a sleeping room and kitchen, a detention cell and a firetruck stall; he also requested that the restrooms be made accessible from outside entrances and perhaps the lobby.[105] Of these suggestions, the detention cell and exterior accessible restrooms were provided.

In April 1956, the *Billings Gazette* reported, "The public use building at Canyon, measuring 110,000 cubic feet, will contain a huge information and orientation station with Yellowstone Park constructed in miniature as a guide for tourists. Restrooms for the public are to be provided in the basement."[106] This description was generally accurate, except that the restrooms were ultimately located on the first floor, along with six offices, a large exhibit room, a post office and an auditorium that seated two hundred. The basement contained a photographer's darkroom, two detention cells, storage rooms and a workshop. In-depth interpretation was not provided.

All of these functions were contained within a one-story building with two nearly identically sized parallel, yet shifted, wings (seventy-six feet long by forty feet wide) that met at the building's center lobby. The south wing held the offices and the north wing the auditorium, as indicated by the continuous wall of glazing at the offices and the solid concrete block walls of the north wing. The building's low-sloped front-gable roof faced the parking lot to the east and extended out deeply to protect the full-height curtain wall flanked by solid walls finished with vertical wood siding. The remaining solid walls and base of the building were finished with red and tan shades of split-face (pumice) block set in running bond.[107]

The design prompted some discussion between YNP's Superintendent Garrison and the WODC architects. Garrison was concerned about the exterior and interior colors being applied to the building; he inquired as to whether WODC had instituted a new color policy that YNP was not aware of. Apparently, the new colors were pastel in tone, whereas Garrison wanted to know "if it is still practical to use exterior colors which are softer and more harmonious with the surroundings." Garrison decided to have only the prime coat applied that fall, allowing time to select the appropriate colors. He requested that YNP be allowed to view the final colors and that perhaps a color expert should visit the site and offer guidance.[108]

When the construction was awarded to Copp Construction of Billings, Montana, in October 1956, the building was to be ten thousand square feet and have a two-hundred-seat auditorium and an administrative office, for a construction cost of $295,060. When completed in time for the August 17, 1958 dedication ceremony, the final cost was $340,000. After its first open season (1959), staff reported that the center fulfilled their expectations: it was conveniently located and adequately sized (though taxed during peak visitor hours), the rooms were conveniently arranged and visitor reaction had been favorable.[109]

The wood shake treatment on the building's roof was similar to that on earlier Park buildings, with every tenth shingle course doubled up. This practice had been used in the Park since the mid-1910s and was probably well received by Park officials. The low slope and rough wood shakes, however, didn't shed snow easily, and the roof structure was inadequate to hold the weight. The shakes were replaced with sheet metal roofing in the early 1990s, yet snow continued to accumulate on the roof. Lower ceilings were added to the auditorium and lobby ceilings to retain heat in what was considered an inefficient, uninsulated building. Over time, NPS found that visitors wanted more space for interpretative exhibits and stores with educational books. These were being packed into the visitor center's lobby, crowding visitors and staff at the information desk. Because the design did not provide for expansion and the deficiencies were deemed too numerous to overcome, the Park demolished most of the visitor center in 2004 and constructed a new one in 2007.

The new Canyon Visitor Center design—by CTA Architects Engineers of Billings, Montana—was vetted through the rigors of Section 106 consultation with the Wyoming State Historic Preservation Office as a form of mitigation for removing the original Mission 66 building, designated a

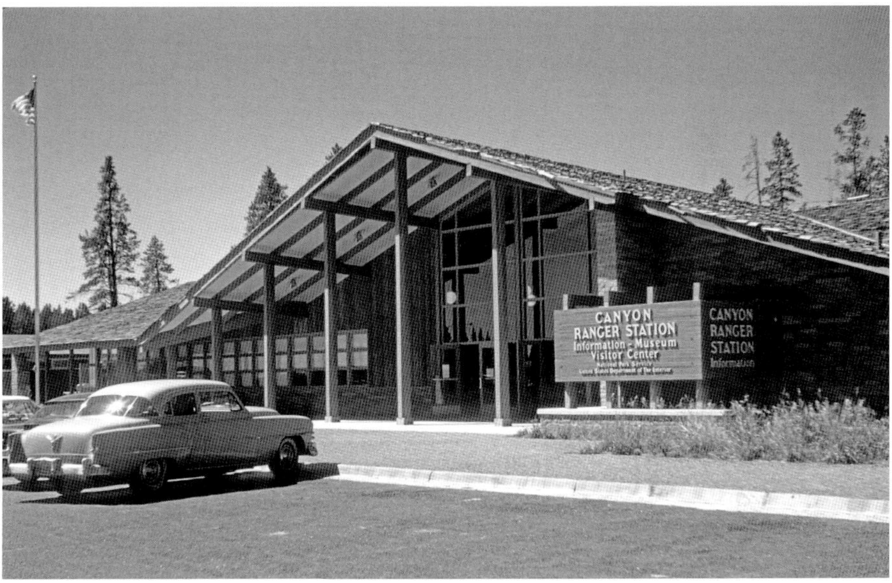

The Canyon Visitor Center design incorporated a large glazed wall facing the lobby, a design feature used at many of the Mission 66 visitor centers. This east-facing entry was protected with a deep roof overhang, 1958. *Courtesy of George and Kathryn Bornemann Yellowstone Collection.*

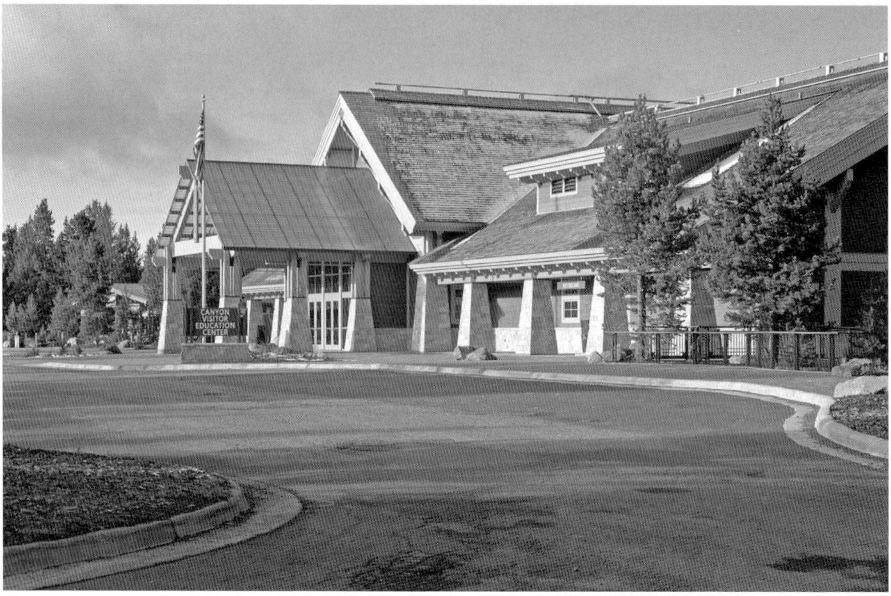

The 2007 Canyon Visitor Center, as designed by CTA Architects Engineers in the Arts and Crafts style. The new building incorporates part of the foundation and part of the auditorium of the original visitor center. *Courtesy of CTA Architects Engineers.*

contributing feature of a potential historic district. The associated 2001 Environmental Assessment prepared by YNP stated that the new building "reflects and melds the Mission 66 architectural philosophy, which embodied a manufactured, 'modern' appearance, and the architectural philosophy of the Arts and Crafts period, which was reflected in the Canyon Hotel… Exposed posts and beams would be sawn and squared, and the siding would be either smooth, sawn cedar shingles or solid wood panels broken with wood cross-trim. The base of the building and pillars would be cut stone. The steeply pitched roof would be covered with sawn cedar shingles."[110]

Canyon Dormitories

YPC originally planned on providing two dormitories for staff. Additional rooms were being provided in the lower level of the lodge and in the east extension of the Administration Building. After the June 26, 1956 construction estimate prompted project revisions and a size reduction of the Administration Building, YPC decided to build three identical dormitories for its staff: two women's dorms and one men's dorm. WB&A's June 8, 1956 drawings would suffice for all three.

It was estimated that five hundred people would be on staff upon completion of the development. Each two-story building was 216 feet long by 29.75 feet wide, 18 feet tall and capped with a low-sloped (1:12) gable roof that paralleled the length of the building. These wood-framed buildings had a simple layout with 13- by 12-foot rooms. The twenty-seven rooms were on either side of the double-loaded corridor, interspersed with a centrally located interior exit stair and two bathroom blocks. Double occupancy allowed each building to house up to 112 staff members.

The building exteriors' clearly reflected the twenty-six-feet, ten-inch structural framing bays, with columns expressed by two- by three-inch battens between the alternating areas of wood siding and of glazing set above plywood panels. The vertical siding was stained, leaving the wood grain visible even from a distance. All the wood is now painted. The extended eaves of the roof typically hold the snow away from the walls.

These simple buildings were parallel to one another, spaced approximately sixty-six feet apart. This distance was discussed during a design conference with

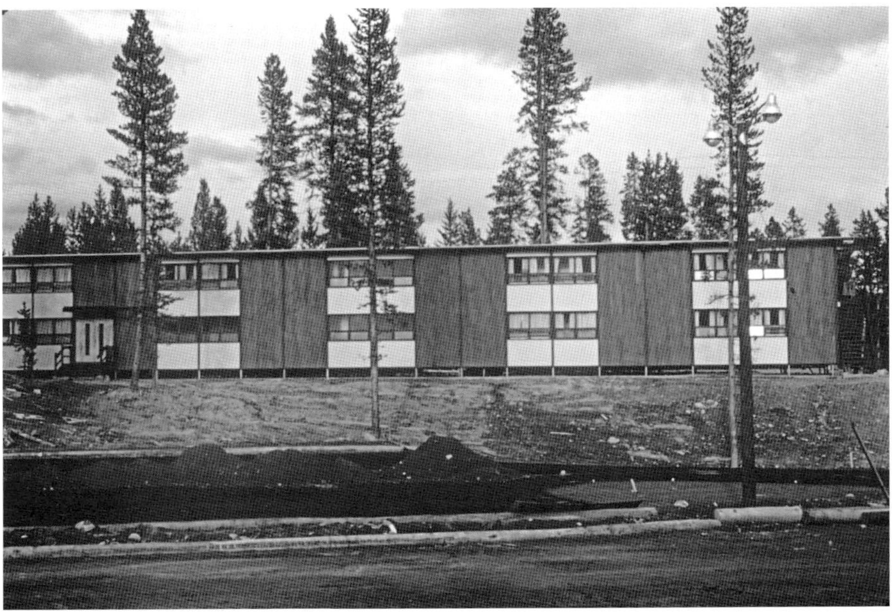

The structural system of the Canyon Village dormitories was clearly expressed in their exterior treatment, 1957. *Photo by Haynes Studios Inc., courtesy of MHS RCPA Haynes Foundation Collection.*

the architect in early 1956, when YPC was planning for just two dormitory buildings. Mattson opined, "Trouble appeared to arise from the 200-foot long dormitory buildings which were being located on terrain which could not readily hold them. This the writer summed up with the statement that the space was there if they were satisfied with placing buildings a little closer together than 80 to 100 feet when our minimum code spacing was forty feet. It also presented a challenge to the designer."[111] The building locations were adjusted accordingly.

Canyon Cabins

YNP's Mission 66 prospectus (compiled in consultation with YPC) had planned for three classes of cabins and no hotels. "It should be noted there are no additional hotels proposed in this program, the economics of which are marginal, they normally are not what the park visitor desires and they are not in complete harmony with park use."[112] Instead, three classes of cabins would be provided: Cottage Class A, with higher-quality finishes and highest rental rate; Lodge Class B, with standard finishes and base rate; Economy Class C, to be rented both furnished and unfurnished at a reduced rate. Class A and B cabins would have a bath or shower, and Class C cabin renters would use the central shower facilities. Each cabin was set up on pipe stilts, and the open bases were to be screened off and covered with cement plaster. Class A and B cabins were ultimately constructed.

The Canyon Village cabins became the financial linchpin of the project for YPC. The project initially included 300 units until the construction cost estimate was exceeded in June 1956. At that critical stage in the project, YPC increased the number of cabin rooms to 512 and postponed the construction of the Recreation Hall. This was a strategy to increase the income more quickly, in order to finance the rest of the project and the others to come.

In response to the short construction season in the Park, McNeil Construction prefabricated cabin parts—wall panels, floors and roofs—in shops in the town of Gardiner, Montana, near the north entrance to the Park. The parts were shipped down to the Canyon site when weather permitted. This construction method affected the design of the buildings. The design was also limited by the eight-room maximum stated in the NPS design manual. A mock-up was made for review by the design team and NPS in early March 1956. Once approved, McNeil would be able to

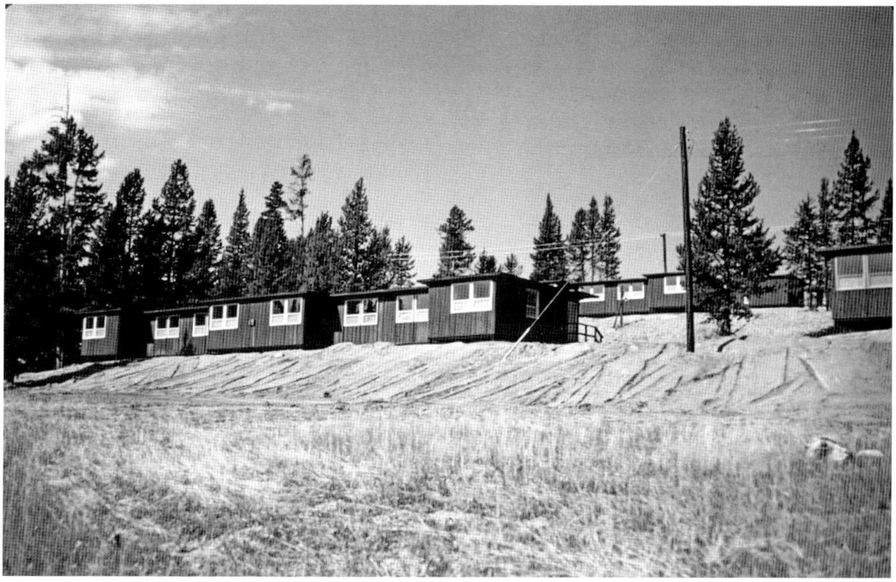

The modular fabrication of the cabins (Cabin Type A) was evident in their appearance, 1957. *Photo by Haynes Studios Inc., courtesy of MHS RCPA Haynes Foundation Collection.*

proceed in earnest and fabricate four cabins each day.[113] The cabins were classified as motel rooms, each of which was typically twelve feet wide; length varied from fourteen to twenty feet.

Two primary cabin designs were used in Loop A and Loop C, identified on the drawings as Cabin Areas A and C. The designs were classified as Cabin Type A—Row Unit, which ganged eight units in a 106-foot-long row. The two end and two center units were 24 feet, 7¼ inches long; the four sandwiched units were 18 feet long. The Cabin Type C—Center Unit design was a mirrored splay of four units each, three of which had three outside walls. Both configurations provided for a mixture of two double-bed units, two single-bed units and one double-bed unit. The details for each type were similar and based on building modules constructed of 2x4's and 4- by 8-foot plywood sheets. The wall panels were identified on the construction drawings and ranged in width from 5 feet, 6¾ inches to 19 feet, 8⅞ inches long; all were 8 feet, 2½ inches high. There were thirty-three panel configurations. Cabin Type C became known as a Frontier Cabin and Cabin A as the Pioneer Cabin.

The interiors were configured and finished simply. Each unit had a bedroom with one or two beds, a desk, a lavatory and adjacent small wardrobe/luggage area (which was added after NPS design review).

The bathrooms had a toilet and a small shower unit. Doors between units created suites as desired. The walls were finished with ⅜-inch-thick plywood finished with sprayed Zolatone paint for durability; the wood base—routed out for electrical runs—was stained. The 3- by 10-inch roof beams and 2- by 6-inch tongue-and-groove decking were exposed as the ceiling and stained. Vinyl tile was laid on the ⅝-inch "Plyscore" subfloor. All walls, floors and ceiling/roofing panels were insulated. The nearly flat roof was of four-ply built-up membranes covered with gravel and hung 18 to 24 inches beyond the wall planes. Identification panels were mounted at an exterior wall of each individual unit.[114] Each unit was constructed on 4- by 8-inch wood girders supported by 2-inch galvanized pipes cast into 12-inch-diameter concrete footings.

Frank Mattson's memoranda to the Park superintendent provide the most detailed information about the design process, which he effected. In February 1956, he described the cabin design generally: "The cabins are to have rough sawn or re-sawn 1" and 10" vertical board with 1 x 3 battens outside which will be stained brown. Inside walls are to be hard

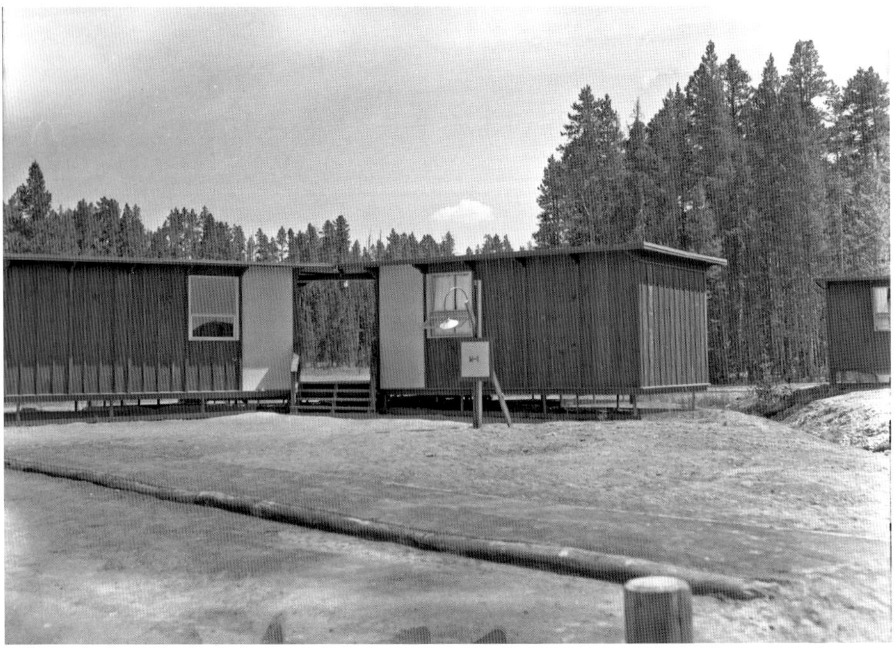

The two-inch-diameter galvanized pipes that were set in twelve-inch-diameter concrete footings and supported the heavy timber girders of the cabins are visible below the cabin body, August 8, 1958. *Photo by Jack E. Boucher, courtesy of NPS, YNP, YELL 29673-3.*

pressed Masonite and painted. Floors will be wood and covered with asphalt tile. Concrete floors are not being used because of the cost of local aggregates."[115] Mattson also provided direction on the colors, noting that light brown was a preferable exterior color because it would darken as it weathered. One continuous interior color was preferred in lieu of distinctly darker battens, which accentuated the panel construction. Use of thinner battens (one by three inches, instead of two by three inches) further de-accentuated the panel system. Additionally, the window sash and trim were to be colored rather than white. It was also agreed that larger bedrooms would be provided in the perimeter units.[116] The cabin doors were color-keyed for quick identification.[117]

The coloration of the cabins was a matter of taste and subsequent discussion. The YNP superintendent wrote to his counterpart at Glacier National Park, "It is believed the stain is too dark with additional trim accents on vertical boards and joists black. Window trim and doors are painted strong hues of red, yellows and blue-greens."[118] Early color images depict these saturated colors at the identification panels, doors and windows.

Design Theory and Past Projects

Welton Becket & Associates

Welton Becket & Associates brought its vast experience with the modern aesthetic to the Canyon Village project. The designs reflected a sure hand, a practiced understanding of working with modules, a knowledge of available and appropriate materials and the ability to produce the many documents required to construct this large complex in just six months. Like many architects, the firm tried to push the design into a more impressive realm, which it toned down in response to the clients (both YPC and NPS) and the budgetary constraints. Becket was known for attending to his clients' wishes, stating in a 1958 interview, "Some architects design to suit their own fancies and costs skyrocket and there is no functionalism." "We design for the client," he later said. "I see no reason why I should express Welton Becket."[119]

The enormity of this design task was appreciated by the supervising architect at WODC. Lyle E. Bennett's review of WB&A's plans for the project was air-mailed in late August 1956, noting the delay in reviewing and approving the plans while "realizing that the architectural firm doing the work has had to perform a complex task in a minimum of time and that private architects are not accustomed to working under the codes recognized by the Service."[120] The comments—regarding the documents for the lodge, the dormitories, Hamilton Store and Dormitory and the motel cabins—applied primarily to mechanical and safety details, electrical items, utilities and so on. These items required close coordination with the various trades and the Park's systems. The speed and complexity of the design probably contributed to the estimating error discovered at the time of the groundbreaking in June 1956. This unfortunate circumstance was apparently new to Becket, who was known for accurate estimating.

WB&A's firm brochure from 1954 spoke of why Welton Becket had been made an AIA Fellow in 1951, specifically citing that he "has consistently produced work which has represented original, arresting and practical solutions to diverse and frequently difficult design problems….As a pioneer in lightweight construction techniques in commercial building nominee has been instrumental in gaining wide acceptance for these techniques which have resulted in considerable savings of deadweight, critical materials and structural costs." All of these attributes, along with the full-service capabilities of his firm—touted as "Total Design, from dishes to heavy construction"—factored into the firm's ability to not only handle this project but also provide a design worthy of the project's stature.[121]

Canyon Village was WB&A's first foray (of only two) into design in the national parks, yet its prior experience with shopping centers (Stonestown and Los Altos, among others) and large Hilton hotels (in Havana and Cairo) demonstrated its ability to design large complexes and respond to a variety of climates. However, although it designed the Hart Albin Department Store in Billings, Montana, in 1953, it had not designed in heavy snow country like Yellowstone.

At the time WB&A was designing Canyon Village, Welton Becket was serving as a consultant for the Air Force Academy in Colorado Springs, Colorado, the striking design of which might have influenced and informed the firm's design for Canyon Village Lodge. WB&A's interior and graphic designs were indicative of the period in their abstract nature and colorful mosaic-type gleam. Many of the firm's projects featured large exterior or interior murals similar to what it designed for the prominent walls in Canyon Village Lodge.

William E. Grabow

Bill Grabow—based in a city (Bozeman) of similar, yet less severe, climate as the Park—was better equipped to design for the snow conditions at Canyon Village. He brought the design sensibility that had been nurtured by modernist architects in the architecture program at Montana State College and also by Fred Willson and Ozzie Berg, with whom he had worked after graduation.

In 1956, Grabow was involved in the joint design venture between Fred Willson and Ozzie Berg for the design of the largest wood (glu-lam) dome in the world, at the time, for the field house at Montana State College (now Montana State University). Grabow administered the construction of this large project, seeing it to completion in 1957. Upon Willson's death in 1956, Grabow took over Willson's firm and many of its repeat clients.[122]

Stone & Glass Ltd.

The furnishings were designed or procured, delivered and installed by Stone & Glass Ltd. (S&G), a firm founded by Douglas Stone and his partner, Glass, in December 1956.[123] Huntley Child Jr. of YPC initiated the contract with S&G on December 15, 1956, with a $20,000 deposit check, engaging it to purchase furniture and design special fixtures for the Canyon Village cabins and lodge. S&G designed, procured and arranged for shipping of the clocks in the lounge and cafeteria; the drapes in the lodge; the beauty and barbershop chairs and dryers; and the furniture for the lodge's dining room, cafeteria, bar, lounge, the dormitories and the cabin motel rooms. It provided the full range of items, from dining chairs to waste baskets and candles to carpets and bed frames. The total contract with S&G amounted to $241,716, including shipping and freight, as well as design fees.

Unfortunately, the relationship between YPC and S&G soured in late 1957 over a $2,700 billing error. This worsened throughout 1958 over a $20,000 freight bill that S&G thought was excessive. YPC was dragged into the Allied Van Lines lawsuit because one of its employees had signed for the shipment in question.[124]

Chapter 5
MISSION 66 MODERNIST DESIGN FEATURES

The history of modern architecture is complex both intellectually and visually and has been the subject of extensive scholarship.[125]
—Theodore H.M. Prudon

Design Philosophy

The planning for Canyon Village began in the 1930s, and the architectural design styles evolved with each ensuing iteration to increasingly reflect the modern era. As part of Mission 66, NPS director Wirth encouraged planners and architects to follow the tenets of modernistic design. Concurrently, he stressed the overarching desire to protect the parks while providing higher levels of visitor use and comfort.

The first tenet to disregard precedent had been a primary driver during the early stages of the modern movement in Europe in the 1930s. Woven with programs designed to improve social conditions and quickly rebuild the cities ravaged during World War I, early modernism took advantage of the industrial advances in material production and construction methods. A democratization of healthy built environments—for working and living—to be available for all led to design that focused on functionality and economy. The ability to use materials with greater spanning capacity and lighter weight created massing, volumes and detailing vastly different from the load-bearing masonry structures of the prior centuries. This excitement

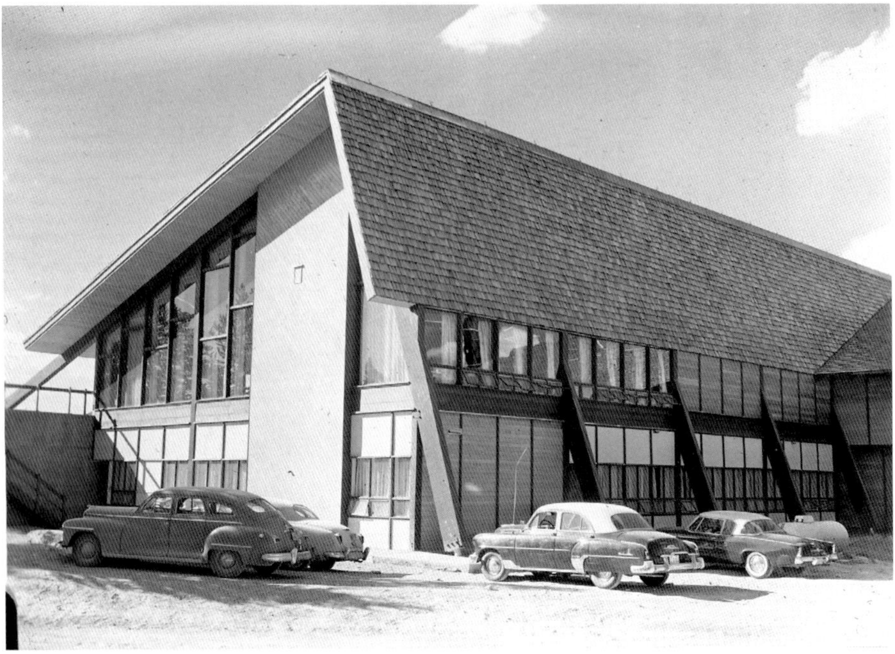

The construction of Canyon Village Lodge made full use of the technological advances that allowed for production of the ninety-two-foot-long glu-lam beams that resulted in a large volume and large expanses of glass, circa 1957. *Courtesy of NPS, YNP, YELL 199116-108.*

of experimentation infused the designs required for a similar movement of extensive building in the United States, in response to factory and housing needs associated with World War II. This need expanded after the war, making up for the diversion to the war effort; returning veterans, restored monetary security and exploding business opportunities spurred on the construction industry. The now more-tested methods of newer construction materials speeded construction.

Modern architecture had become mainstream by the time NPS was planning Mission 66 projects. NPS architects and their consultants were well versed in the modern architectural language, which brought startling simplicity, volumetric clarity, lack of ornament and large expanses of glass to the parks. Unlike much of the modern architecture outside the parks, the visible use of steel was still considered anathema to the naturalness inherent in the parks. The Canyon Village designs straddled the modern and the old worlds—partly because the buildings were flanked by forests and not a modern, fast-paced downtown city and partly because the Park's landscape architect directed the designs to reflect the natural conditions of Yellowstone. This resulted in roof slopes and materials that shed snow but could support the weight of the snow that was held on the roofs, as well as the use of natural materials such as stone and wood. Within these stricter Park parameters, WB&A's designs incorporated newer technologies, such as the glu-lam beams, large panes of plate glass and prefabricated parts. The latter technique enabled off-site production (unhampered by the short construction season) of the cabin parts. In the United States, experimentation with prefabrication for war-related construction was applied in the postwar period to housing and other public buildings.

The Park Service's forward thinking was tempered at first by a desire for the buildings to be of service and to not be the attraction. The buildings were not to compete with the natural features, which were the raison d'etre of the parks. As noted by Ethan Carr in his extensive analysis of Mission 66, "In 1954 Conrad Wirth had famously rejected Frank Lloyd Wright as the architect for a new restaurant in Yosemite Valley. Wirth derided Wright's proposal as a 'mushroom-dome type of thing,' a 'thing to see, instead of being for service.' The very next year, however, Wirth dedicated the Jackson Lake Lodge, and at the same time his own design offices, the WODC and EODC, were producing modernist designs, some of which continued to startle and occasionally outrage at least some critics."[126] Soon after, NPS was praised for showing "the courage, if that's what it is, to accept the design for a pavilion at Dinosaur National Monument, done by Anshen & Allen....As architects have pointed out, the continual effort to pretend a building isn't there only makes it the more prominent, by guaranteeing that it will not be designed to belong there."[127]

The architectural design community embraced this form of thinking. As noted by architect Eldridge Spencer, designer of Colter Bay Visitor Center in Grand Teton National Park:

> *Architectural styles usually become an organization of motifs and lose their essential ability to define space. Overworked, decadent styles have no place in a National Park. Particularly in the Parks heavy arbitrary restrictive massive architectural motifs should not be used to define space; we can and should handle the design without such exaggeration. We have inherited the desire for mass and solidity from our European background. Public taste and our designers should be freed from this influence.*[128]

The Park Service was treading a fine line during the production of Mission 66, as it needed to satisfy critics representing various interests—primarily conservation, architecture, function and budget. In terms of function, NPS was providing new and modern types of facilities. The different uses led to different typologies for the parks—motels, not hotels, as well as visitor centers.

The Park Service published booklets with questions and answers about Mission 66, hoping to disseminate the driving factors that produced the new construction visitors would see in the parks. To answer what type of visitor accommodations were being developed, NPS proffered:

> *The trend of development will be to modern, multi-unit, motel-type accommodations in a price range to meet all reasonable demands. No more large hotels of the type built in many parks in earlier years will be built under Mission 66, as the needs of visitors on wheels will be satisfied more adequately by motel-type units. Modern, fully equipped trailer parks will be developed by concessioners in areas where such facilities are needed.*[129]

NPS further explained that the multi-unit structures would be of economical design and that savings would be passed on to the visitor. Yellowstone NPS staff felt strongly that Canyon Village should be of one vocabulary and that the buildings should harmonize with one another. This expression became known throughout the parks as "Park Service Modern."

Massing and Volume

Welton Becket's designs at Canyon Village exemplified the simplicity and clarity attributed to modern design. The original design parameters were announced in the *Billings Gazette* in May 1956 in anticipation of the construction that would begin the next month: "All the public buildings are of heavy timber construction with high gable roofs, sheer glass walls and some native stone to be used for exterior facings. The large lodge building and recreation hall will feature heavy laminated beam high gable roofs."[130]

The massing of the lodge and the companion Administration Building are dissimilar, reflecting their different functions and their relationship to each other. The voluminous lodge, with primary space 320 feet long by 62 feet wide, was configured like a bank barn, built into the hillside. The first

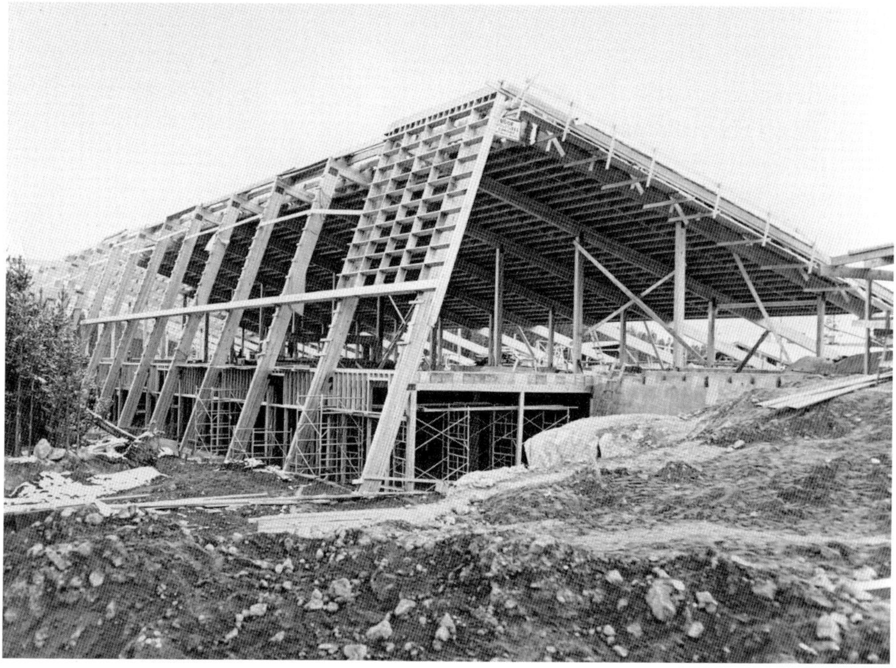

The 1956 construction photograph of Canyon Village Lodge, from the northeast, illustrated the bank barn–type of split-level cross-section of the building. *YPC photo, courtesy NPS, YNP, YELL 185385-57.*

floor area was akin to a ski lodge, with 27-foot tall soaring spaces within the large volume enabled by the glu-lam beams noted above. The layout was logical, based on the regular 20-foot spacing of the glu-lams that rose from the exterior grade—where they were held down expressively by concrete thrustblocks—up to the high ridge beam that spanned the full length of the building. The primary roof was of two different slopes—the west slope gentler as it protected only the upper floor and the east slope steep as it precipitated down to the lower grade. This configuration was further articulated and exaggerated by the location of the ridge beam just 8 feet from the east wall. This off-center location created an expressive and dynamic volume with actively sloping beams, end walls increasing in height and large ceiling areas offset by sizable expanses of glass. A single column line of glu-lam timbers, in approximate mid-span of the long west roof slope, marched the regular 20-foot rhythm down the length of the building, providing support for the glu-lam beams as well as the gift shop wall. The 8-foot, 3-inch height of the translucent gift shop walls floated low below the

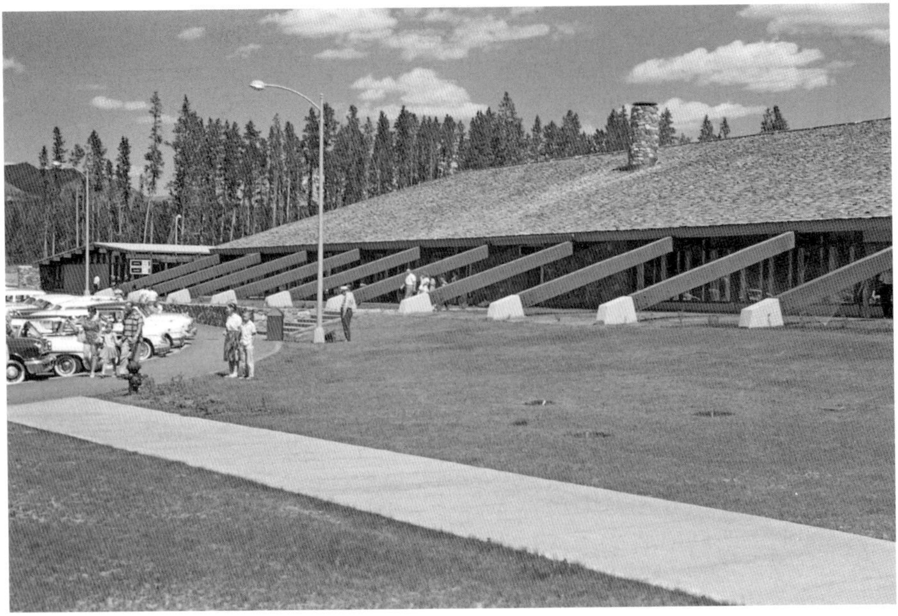

Canyon Village Lodge presented what appeared to be a single-volume space, with variances in texture of the selected materials, 1957. *Courtesy of George and Kathryn Bornemann Yellowstone Collection.*

vastness of the lounge space. This volume was penetrated only by the round stone fireplace chimney and adjacent restrooms.

This primary space was intersected by the east kitchen wing, which, in accordance with its supportive function, had a lower gable roof that engaged the east slope of the main lodge space. Under this intersection, a mezzanine effectively squashed the serving functions below an eight-foot-high ceiling. The mezzanine area was originally designed to include public restrooms that would be accessed by stairs at the north end of the coffee shop. A screen wall, the full eighty-foot length of the west face of this mezzanine, was to provide a feeling of openness to the four-foot, eight-inch-wide hallway beyond.[131] This dramatic height variance, and the interior mass (and originally intended translucency) of the mezzanine, further emphasized the openness of the long public areas north and south of it. These simple design moves, which were in direct response to the functions, had a huge impact on the feel of the space.

The massing of Hamilton's Store was designed in a similar vein, like a bank barn set into the hillside that defined the perimeter of the commercial area of the village. The store's cross-section was less dynamic than the lodge's, with a center ridge beam supported by glu-lam beams spaced twenty

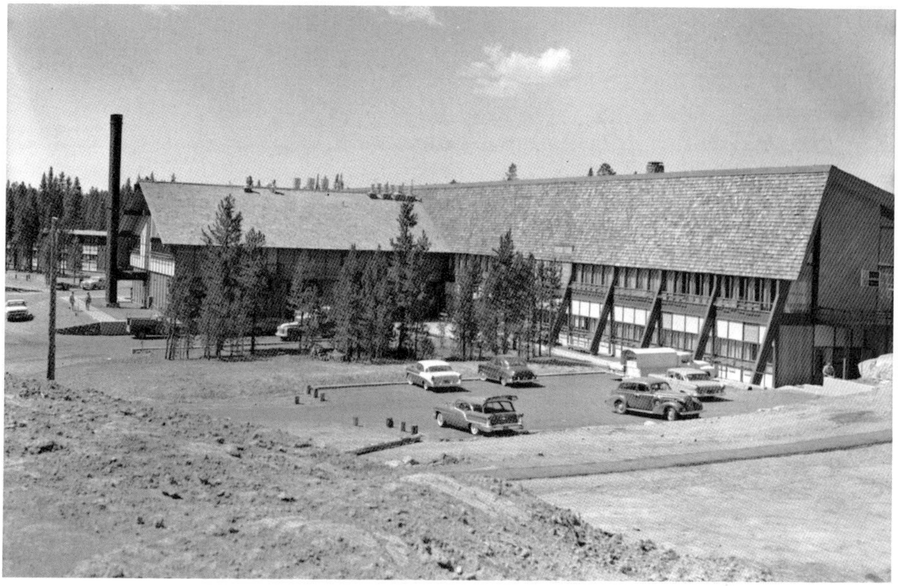

The mass of the kitchen wing, *at left*, penetrated the east part of Canyon Village Lodge at the coffee shop area, August 1958. *Photo by Jack E. Boucher, courtesy of NPS, YNP, YELL 29672-4.*

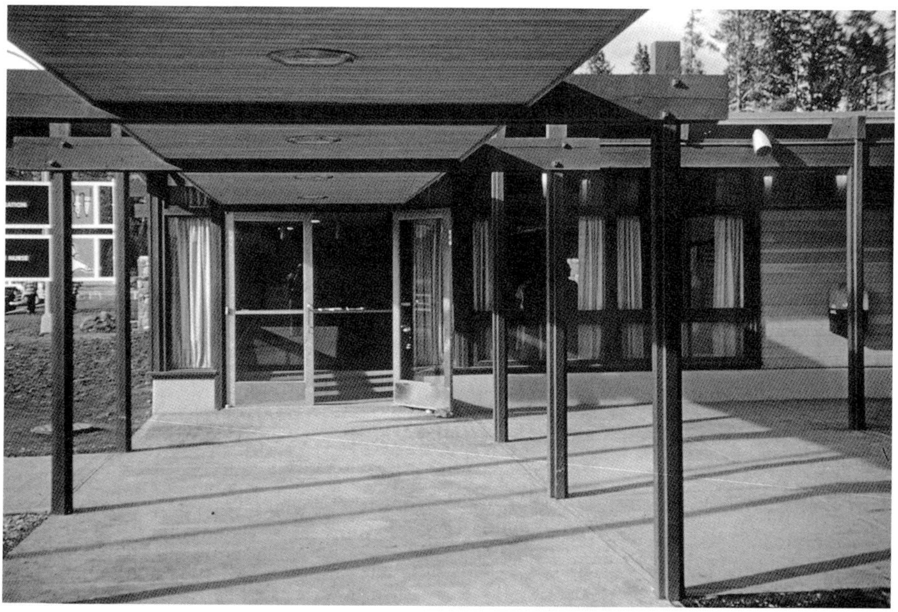

The covered walkway extended from Canyon Village Lodge into the Administration Building to the north, where it transformed into a soffit, 1957. *Photo by Haynes Studios Inc., courtesy of MHS RCPA Haynes Foundation Collection.*

feet apart. The large volume of the grade-level retail space was unbroken for its nearly two-hundred-foot length. The ridge beam, at twenty-two feet above the floor level, and exposed glu-lam beams expressed the structure. These beams did not extend to grade on either side of the building; instead, they extended out to provide eight-foot, six-inch-deep protective eaves along the north and south walls of the building.

The expression of structure—particularly in the ninety-two-foot-long glu-lam beams of the lodge—was intended to boast the modern capabilities and honestly show how the buildings were constructed. This strong feature of modernism—honesty in structure—was in direct response to what had been perceived as contrivances in prior designs. The large wall areas composed of glazing allowed for this expression to be clearly read.

Welton Becket's hierarchy of design—as expressed in the difference in scale and roof shapes of the buildings—created background buildings of modest simplicity. As noted earlier, the Administration Building was unlike the expression of Canyon Lodge. This much smaller building, at 2,610

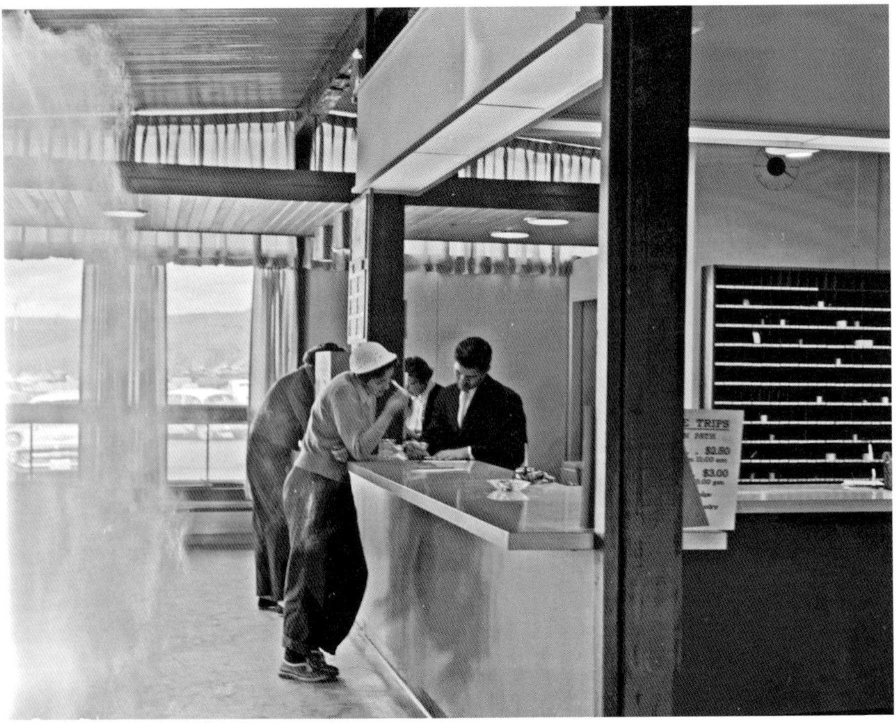

The soffit, which acted as the continuum of the covered walkway, is visible beyond the registrants at the front desk of the Administration Building, August 23, 1957. *Photo by Teisberg, courtesy of NPS, YNP, YELL 29669-2.*

square feet, was nearly square in plan, with a rear corner carved out. The whole was covered with a nearly flat (1:12 pitch) gable roof, with a ridge perpendicular to that of the lodge. The resulting mass is subservient to the lodge it serves to the south. The connecting covered walkway has a common modernistic trend whereby the walkway's roof penetrates into the interior of the building, taking on the form of an interior soffit.

The two-story dormitories are located behind the horseshoe-shaped hill of the commercial area. They are long, plain, nearly flat-roofed wood-framed structures that present an insistent rhythm of solid natural wood wall planes alternating with full-height sections of glazing over spandrels. The cabins were prefabricated in parts, with traditional wood-framing for wall, floor and roof panels. These panels provided for simple cubic massing set either in long rows (the Type A eight-plexes) or in alternating rotations (Type C) that created more visual interest and wall area for windows.

Materials

It is often stated that the materials used in the 1950s were cheap, inexpensive and not durable. This was not pervasive, as fine and durable materials were still available, stemming from their use in the 1930s and 1940s, and not all new materials from the 1950s were substandard. Some of the materials used in Canyon Village were more traditional, such as wood, stone, plaster, ceramic tile and wood shakes. Other materials were indicative of the advances made in technology and fabrication, such as the glu-lam beams and columns, as well as plywood for exterior use. The improvements made in adhesives made these applications possible. The primary structural materials used for the lodge, Administration Building and Hamilton Store were high-quality materials intended to last.

WB&A's design theme for the material selections appears to have been one common to the modernist aesthetic: honest expression of material and contrast between textures and colors. Wood was used extensively, as a natural material at home in the Park and one that provided warmth. It was a trademark feature of the rustic designs of the Park Service Modern style. Three different treatments of exterior wood siding demonstrated the subtle detail that was carefully thought out during design. At the two gable ends of both Canyon Lodge and Hamilton Store, diagonally placed, naturally finished V-groove boards finish the interior and exterior fifteen-foot-wide wall

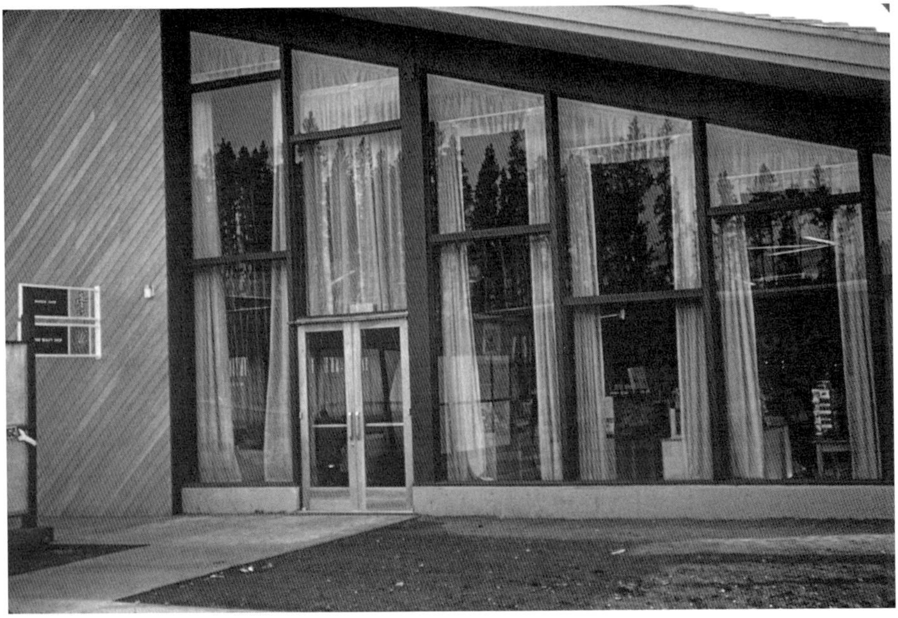

The north end wall of Canyon Village Lodge retained the architect's design preference for full-height glazing, 1957. *Photo by Haynes Studios Inc., courtesy of MHS RCPA Haynes Foundation Collection.*

sections that extend the full height of the interior space. These components visually acted like fireplaces. Where not filled with glazing, wall surfaces on the public sides of the buildings were finished with vertical board siding or stone. The rear of the buildings were finished with horizontal wood boards set in equal sections defined by vertical battens that divided the column spacing into four units.

The plate glass, pervasive at all the walls of the buildings within the commercial area around the parking lot, was set within a stepped wood mullion detail at all three public buildings designed by WB&A. Steel and aluminum were not part of this rustic expression. The early 1955 rendered images by WB&A depict the designer's preference for a more minimal appearance of support at the glazed areas.

The interior materials demonstrate the intended modernistic juxtaposition of materials—smooth and textured, matte and glossy—and highlight the inherent character of each material. Concrete at the fireplace was unpainted, wood wall and ceiling boards were unpainted, the Douglas fir of the end-grain wood block flooring showed red warmth through the clear finish and the smooth fireplace hood gleamed with bright copper. The materials were selected to withstand heavy use and have endured well. These generally basic finishes acted as a neutral backdrop for the color that was introduced into the fixtures and furnishings.

Colors

Color was used as a counterpoint to the neutrality and warmth of the primarily wood background of all WBA's buildings in Canyon Village. This color was expressed mostly in the interiors—in furniture, accent artwork on primary walls, chandeliers and sheer curtains. The modicum of color at the exterior was more noticeable due to its rarity. Cabin doors were painted primary colors to aid in location identification, and the fascias and rakes at the roof edges of both Canyon Lodge buildings and Hamilton Store were painted orange and turquoise, respectively. Images of the site when first opened emphasize the universal popularity of these colors, as they blended in with the colorful cars parked in the lot. The use of color in the project is indicative of the period and reflected modernist design philosophies.

The interior colors were of a family: orange, yellow, turquoise-green and robin's egg blue. These were featured on the starlight fixtures located down the length of Canyon Lodge, creating a color stream just ten feet above the floor. Each fixture in the larger spaces had eight arms of varying lengths; the gift shop fixtures were smaller and sported only six arms. These colors were also reflected in the upholstered couches and arm chairs providing resting spots in the lounge and in the dining room and cafeteria chairs.

The dining room and coffee shop were treated to what has become known as "line art," which was removed in the 1980s. It appears to have been fabricated from one- by four-inch wood strips that were fastened in a variety of shapes to just one wall of the dining room and the wall above the coffee shop. The base color of the dining room wall itself was dark brown or black, setting off the pink, orange, yellow, white and blue figures depicted by the line art. Abstract figures of people holding hands, sunbursts, Indian headdresses and other geometric shapes were simple and striking. Similar figures were mounted to a white background at the large mezzanine wall above the coffee shop. No drawings or references have been found for this work; it was not mentioned in the press releases, although it figured prominently in the 1957 Haynes slides that documented the finished building. Welton Becket & Associates had a well-respected interior design department that created interior and exterior murals on a grand scale; it is probable that it designed this artwork.[132]

Clocks mounted to the far north and south end walls of Canyon Lodge contributed to the overmantel impression of the "fireplace" feature. The north clock, facing the lounge, is a large golden sunburst of elegant expression. The ten-foot-diameter south clock was in the style of George Nelson, with large colorful circles representing the hours and long dark hands pointing to the time. This clock is no longer extant and was not shown on the drawings. Early photographs provide colorful images that depict its large circumference and simplicity.

The most appealing feature of Canyon Lodge was in the cocktail bar, where sophistication reigned. The back bar—some twenty-seven feet long—graced the back south wall behind the bartenders. It was blacklit to provide a luminous blue sea with sparsely located abstractions in orange, light blue, black and white. This controlled the atmosphere in the bar and exuded a perfect cool contrast to the rough stone exterior wall.

Chapter 6
CANYON VILLAGE CONSTRUCTION

For here today, as we break ground for the new Canyon Village, I can actually feel and see that MISSION 66 is at last under way.
—Conrad L. Wirth, director, National Park Service, June 24, 1956

Cabin Prefabrication

Construction of the Canyon Village buildings began with fabrication of the cabin parts. YPC, NPS, the architect and McNeil had met in Gardiner on March 8, 1956, to review the prototypical cabin fabrication and made minor design modifications at that time. Construction began in earnest on April 1, 1956, the day after YPC had secured its $3 million loan. The loan included construction of 300 motel units. The financial success of the project—and YPC's ability to stay afloat as a company—depended on completion and rental of the cabins. When the cost estimate for construction of Canyon Village escalated in June 1956, YPC increased the number of cabin units from 300 to 512. The cost increase to $2.2 million would be offset by the increased income generated from the cabin rental. Two cabin loop roads would be populated with cabins: Loop A, directly south of Hamilton Store, and the larger Loop C east of Canyon Lodge. A small Loop B, located between these two loops, would not receive cabins until 1969. (Cabin type and loop naming were not related; Type A and Type C cabins were at each of the loops.) As cabin installation took place, NPS supervised the site configuration and regrading, as part of its infrastructure scope of work.

Prefabrication consisted of various wall, roof and floor panels, numbered to correspond to locations on the building. To facilitate this, McNeil made jigs that provided for repeated and consistent manufacturing. These parts were made in Gardiner, just outside the north boundary of the Park, and later trucked (during the evening hours)[133] down to the site for assembly on the post foundation supports. McNeil's construction crews arrived in Yellowstone in mid-May 1956.[134] Due to heavy snows, construction on site was delayed until May 25, 1956.[135] The goal was to erect six cabins each day; actual production rate was approximately three and a half cabins per day.

By October 1, 1956, 300 motel cabin units had been erected on site; the heating and hot water systems would be installed in the spring. The remaining 200 units were in various stages of completion, averaging approximately 50 percent. The rushed construction—and slow site preparation—held up erection. Just 100 of these last cabins remained uncompleted in March 1957. As of July 1, 1957—the soft opening day for Canyon Village—150

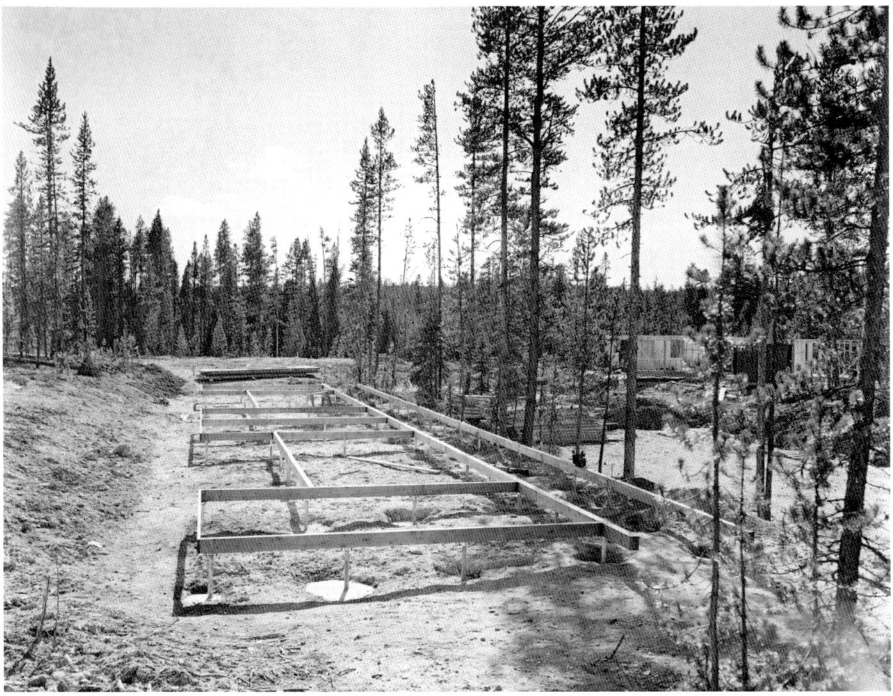

McNeil constructed Type A cabin framing on site to receive the cabin parts. *YPC photo, courtesy NPS, YNP, YELL 185385-60.*

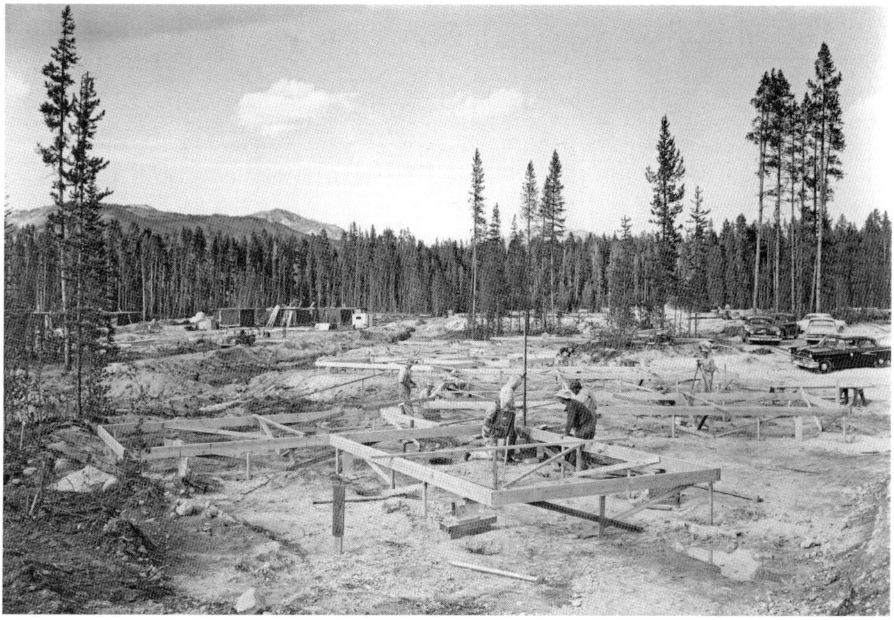

McNeil's crews erected as many cabin supports as possible during the short construction season. Type C cabin framing is visible in the foreground; assembled Type C cabins are visible in the background. *YPC photo, courtesy NPS, YNP, YELL 185385-62.*

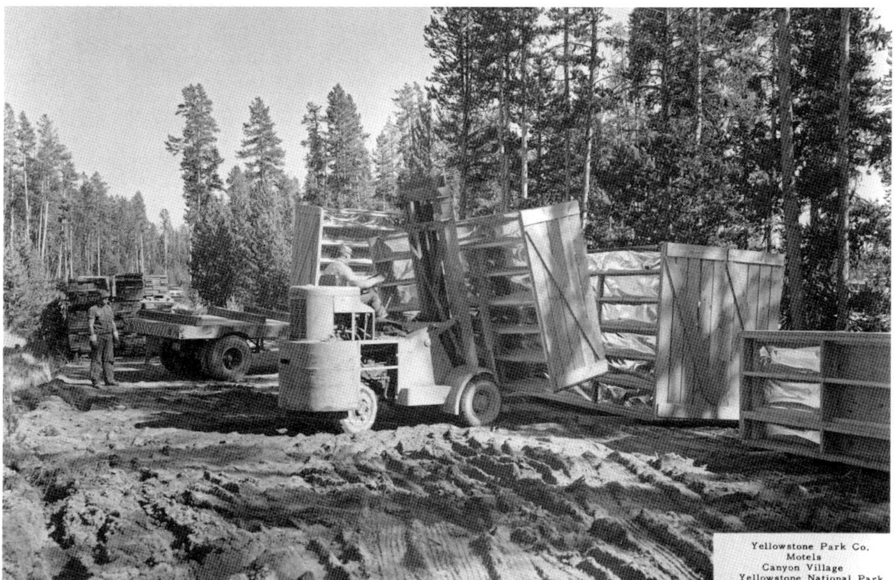

McNeil's crew lifting cabin wall panel for delivery to prepared supports, on September 14, 1956. The mud slowed progress. *YPC photo, courtesy NPS, YNP, YELL 185385-61.*

cabins would be ready in Loop C and 220 in Loop A. Furnishings had been procured and installed by New York firm Stone & Glass Ltd.

Yellowstone's Frank Mattson did not feel that these cabins were well suited to the hillsides where they were located.[136] In late 1958, Yellowstone superintendent Garrison relayed other construction complaints to John Q. Nichols of YPC, primarily related to insufficient soundproofing and heating.[137] Garrison's letter unleashed a ten-page response from Thomas J. Hallin, YPC's director of construction-engineering, to Nichols, who read from his home in La Jolla, California, that the quality of workmanship was generally poor, which they'd been aware of as early as March 1956. Hallin attributed this to lack of interest by the contractor and by the architect (Hallin said he failed to properly inspect construction).

Hallin did admit that "the project was undertaken too rapidly and there were many plan changes made after the initial contract was awarded but the disputes are too numerous."[138] Hallin continued to negotiate with both parties to rectify the deficiencies. The soundproofing was improved with installation of the Celotex panels over the solid wood beams between the adjoining partitions and the roof deck and would be further improved with installation of carpeting in 1959.

The heating system design had been reduced to one large unit for the lodge, Administration Building and the cabins. This cost-saving measure created balancing problems in adjusting heat flow and consistency of heat level (and comfort) between the cabins. This was exacerbated by installation errors, which resulted in lines and valves full of rock and silt, as well as provision of the wrong convectors. The cabin wall, floor and roof parts had been insulated during fabrication, "but the prefabricated floor panels were stored in yards where the insulation absorbed moisture—they found that about 80% of the insulated joist spans contained from 3–5 gallons of water." The result was cold floors that felt even colder without carpeting. The list of construction errors continued on to include the showers, window operators, tile floors ("cracking due to improper installation of the subfloor"), water closets, lavatories and a confusing cabin numbering system. Hallin estimated the cost to rectify the key items would total nearly $120,000.[139]

The YPC board of directors approved the expenditures, considering them necessary to be able to rent the cabins and generate the anticipated income. The improvements gave YPC a 1,550-person capacity in the cabins, with each person charged a daily rate of ten dollars. The hotel rooms at Mammoth and Lake commanded a similar rate. The last cabin loop, "B," was not completed by YPC, despite repeated efforts. YPC's financial struggles

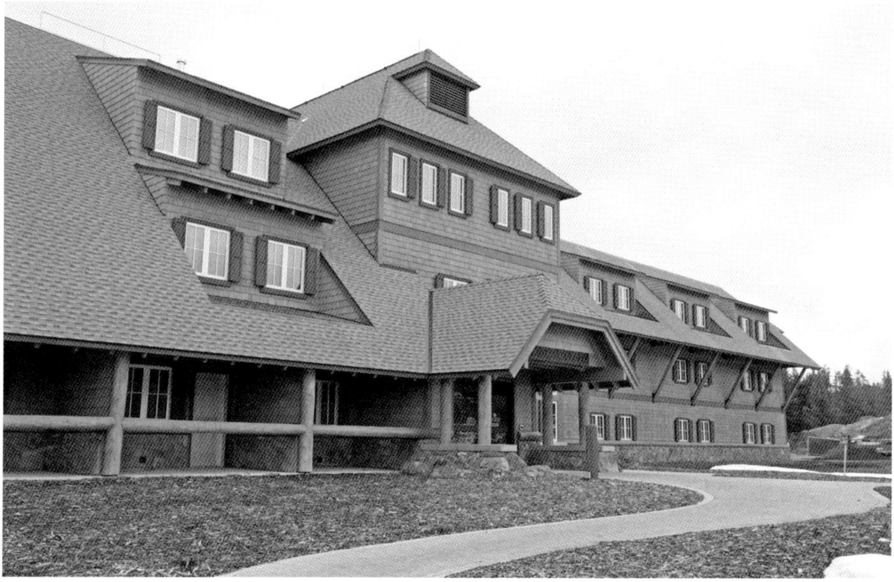

Chittenden Lodge, constructed in 2015, one of the hotels replacing the 512 Canyon Village cabins, in 2016. *Photo by the author.*

caused it to abandon its five-year Capital Improvement and Construction Program, scheduled to begin in 1962. Instead, it asked YNP for permission to continue renting the extant campers' cabins at the old Canyon development. YPC's request in August 1964 presented the following argument:

> *We should like to suggest that, due to the fact no definite plans have been set up these past two years for Area "B" at Canyon Village, the Canyon Campers Cabins be used for another year. We have, I think, pointed out that these cabins are sold 100% for most of the season, mostly unfurnished, and occupied for the most part by fishermen. These cabins, as you know, are sold very cheaply. With the increased traffic in the Park and the need for overnight accommodations, it is most definitely our feeling that these campers cabins are needed for visitors who like to "rough it" and are not looking for so-called deluxe accommodations.*[140]

The cabins in Loop B were not built until 1969, designed and constructed by YPC's successor firm, General Host. The cabins in Loops A and C were demolished as part of the 2014–16 redevelopment of Canyon Village; they have been supplanted with Arts and Crafts–style hotels, representing a full circle away from the motel type of units back to the hotel type.

THE GROUNDBREAKING

The moneymaking cabins were the initial focus of YPC, yet the groundbreaking of Canyon Village Lodge was the moment Conrad Wirth had looked forward to since the initial days of planning Mission 66. It was a concrete expression of the launch of the Park Service's nationwide program to save the parks and gave Wirth a platform to promote specific aspects of the initiative. To direct the tone of the event—and the ensuing press coverage—in May 1956, Wirth provided an outline for all who would be involved in the June 1956 presentation and oversaw all the messages presented. He stressed that the concessioners should be applauded for their "positive approach" to the needed expansion in Yellowstone, that major international architectural and national construction firms were used to implement this Canyon project and that this was a response to increased vacation time and travel. It was neither a "modernization" plan nor "replacement of obsolete facilities."[141]

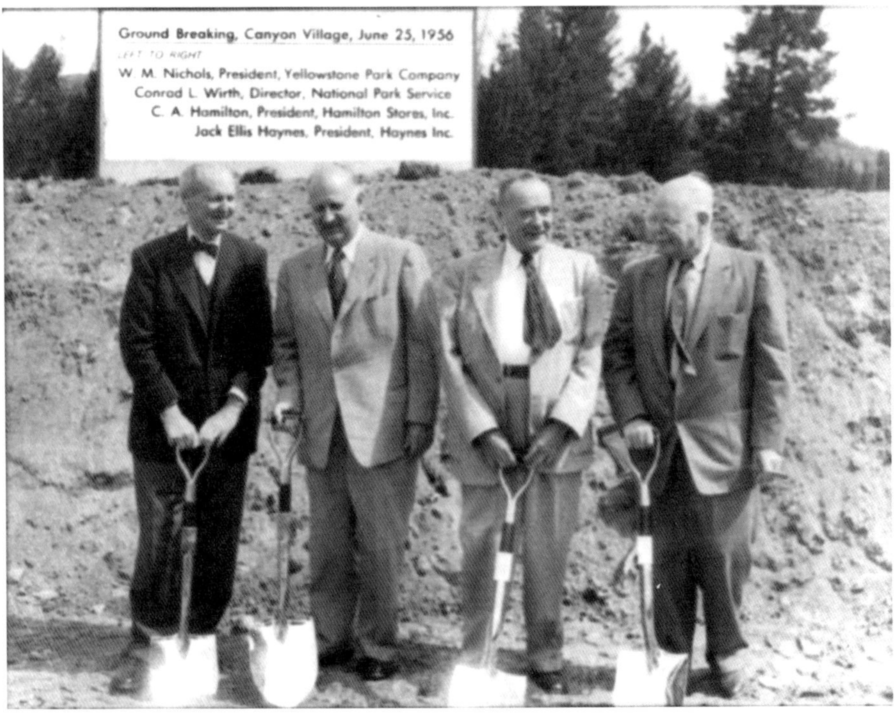

The June 25, 1956 groundbreaking ceremony for Canyon Village Lodge brought together the three prime concessioners at YNP with the director of the Park Service. *From left to right*: William Nichols (YPC), Conrad Wirth (NPS), Charles Hamilton (Hamilton Stores) and Jack Ellis Haynes (Haynes Photo Shops). *Courtesy NPS, YNP, YELL 133563.*

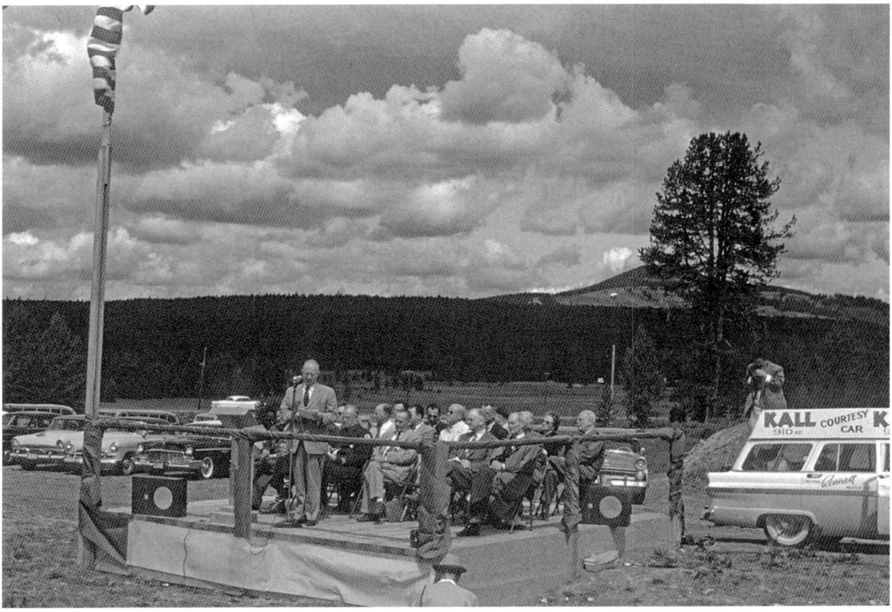

Conrad L. Wirth, director of the National Park Service, speaking at the groundbreaking ceremony for Canyon Village Lodge, June 25, 1956. *Courtesy of George and Kathryn Bornemann Yellowstone Collection.*

One of the Department of the Interior's press releases that announced the groundbreaking on June 24, 1956, clarified the construction project as one of conservation: "When Canyon Village is completed, for instance, we plan to remove all of the structures that over the years have encroached on the rim of the Grand Canyon. Only the hotel will remain in its present location and that, as you know, is some distance from the rim of the Canyon.... The new village will be located in an area some distance back from the canyon rim, screened by woods from the spectacular gorge where the Lower Falls are twice the height of Niagara."[142]

The ceremony occurred over two days, beginning with Saturday evening cocktails at Canyon Hotel, which was to be improved as part of the project.[143] The shovel-wielding ritual took place the next day at 10:00 a.m., at the Canyon Village Lodge site. YNP superintendent Edmund Rogers officiated, both NPS director Conrad Wirth and Assistant Secretary of the Interior Wesley A. D'Ewart spoke and each concessioner (YPC, Hamilton Stores and Haynes Inc.) was introduced. It was fitting that D'Ewart speak, for as a Montana congressman, he had been a passionate supporter of

Yellowstone and other national parks. And Wirth's hard work was coming to fruition, leading him to speak from the heart:

> *This occasion will remain forever as one of the truly great and memorable moments of my lifetime. For here today, as we break ground for the new Canyon Village, I can actually feel and see that Mission 66 is at last under way. The National Park Service has entered a new era which promises to be the most rewarding in its history.*[144]

Further, he placed this beginning of Mission 66 in perspective, by placing it at the first national park where the idea of the National Park Service had been born in 1870:

> *It is altogether fitting that the inaugural ceremony for this great forward-looking program—which provides the tools needed to conserve, protect, and develop the priceless heritage that is our National Park System—should be held here in Yellowstone National Park. For this park is, and always will be, symbolic of the inspiration and the unselfish vision that has gone into the creation and preservation of that System.*[145]

The lengthy list of people and company representatives invited to the groundbreaking reflects the size and importance of the occasion, as well as the new modes of traveling to the park, the funding of the park improvements and the media available. Presidents and managers of oil companies, airlines, bus lines and railroads came; bankers attended; and radio, television and news reporters were invited. It was hoped that the latter would promote this event and explain the nationwide effort to the millions at home. Newspapers around the country covered the event. A full-page spread on the cover of Helena's June 24, 1956 issue of the *Independent Record* included two renderings by WB&A and three photos of natural features (one being the Grand Canyon). The title "Ground Breaking for Canyon Village Opens New Park Era" was supported by the subtitle "Yellowstone Park Development Planned to Cope with Vast Multitudes of Visitors."[146]

Literal ground was broken that day in a shovel ceremony by Wirth, William Nichols (YPC), Charles Hamilton and Jack Haynes. The Park Service had already spent more than $1 million in laying sewer and water lines, parking areas, streets and paths, as well as installing the new campground. This was part of Mission 66's "one package" approach to solving park development projects promoted by Wirth. Gilbert Lord and Griswold Raltze of WB&A, L.G. and Bruce McNeil of McNeil Construction and Superintendent Edmund Rogers held court as well.

THE CONSTRUCTION

McNeil Construction Company had mobilized on site in May 1956 and begun in earnest on May 25, after the snow was cleared. McNeil constructed the buildings for YPC and Hamilton Stores. McNeil Construction, of Los Angeles, California, was accustomed to large projects, having built Disneyland, Sun Valley Lodge, the Lockheed guided missile plant in San Francisco and the Convair guided missile plant in San Diego. Primarily local firms supplied the materials used in the construction. Northwest Fixture Company of Billings provided kitchen fixtures (as it had within the Park since 1912), Simkins Hallin of Bozeman provided general construction materials and Billings Sash and Door provided glazing and doors.[147]

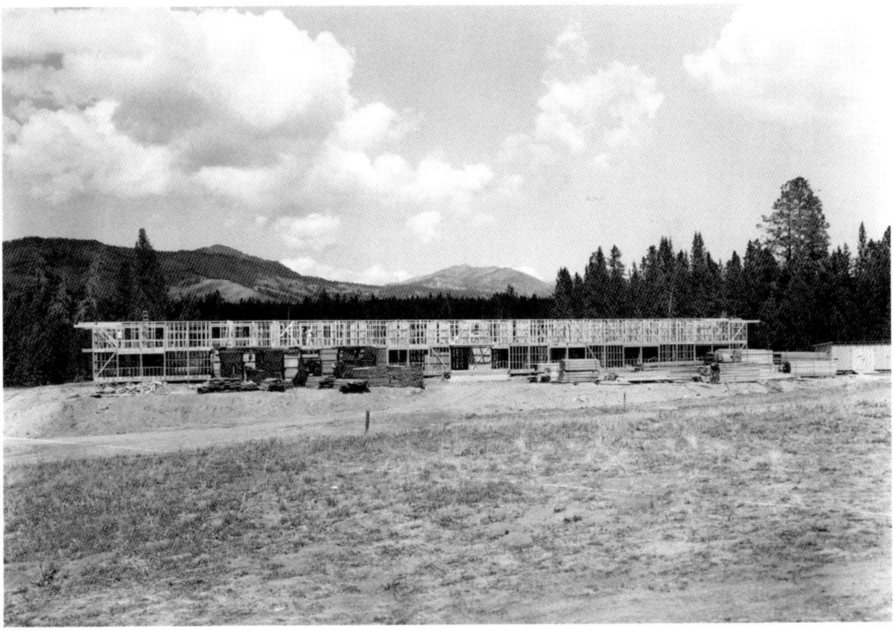

One of YPC's dormitories under construction, 1956. *YPC photo, courtesy NPS, YNP, YELL 185385-58.*

McNeil's contractual construction cost, on July 30, 1956, was $97,219 for the Administration Building and $1,208,317 for Canyon Village Lodge. The total contract—including the 512 motel units, the Administration Building, lodge and three dormitories—was $4,017,138, plus a 7 percent fee of $321,371, for a total of $4,338,509.[148] As of March 1958, the final construction cost had increased to $5.6 million.[149]

Local contractors were awarded the Park Service contracts, which was of interest to the local newspapers. Long Construction of Billings, Montana, received the $553,132 road construction contract, which included reconstruction and paving of the obsolete roads in the Park, as well as paving of the Canyon Village parking area and 11.84 miles of the Grand Loop Highway between Lake and Canyon Junctions.[150] Cop Construction Company of Billings was the successful low bidder for construction of the visitor center, a utility building and six other buildings. Its contract was for $655,087.50. The electrical system at Canyon was provided for $100,000 and a reservoir installed for $112,870.[151]

The last NPS contract for Mission 66 work at Canyon Village was announced on December 20, 1956. Studer Construction Company of Billings bid $216,004 for the base coursing, surfacing and construction of log curbing on the roads, parking areas and walks in the concessioner's cabin area, as well as the government employees' trailer court.[152] The late timing of this contract and subsequent construction meant that Studer's crew would be finalizing site grading during and after erection of the cabins.

Site Development Challenges

The Canyon Village area is at an elevation of 7,734 feet and is subject to heavy, deep snows and freezing temperatures at all months of the year. These conditions, in conjunction with a short construction schedule and the tensions associated with the national attention focused on the project, resulted in delays, construction failures and finger-pointing.

Soils in the area are "derived from rhyolitic sands and gravels that were originally deposited as glacial till."[153] These soils were problematic during construction, as relayed by YPC to its attorney, in its effort to hold NPS responsible for uneven site conditions in the cabin areas. The "recent glaciation and a conservable amount of glacial till (unstratified drift such as clay, sand, gravel and boulders) was deposited over various formations....In

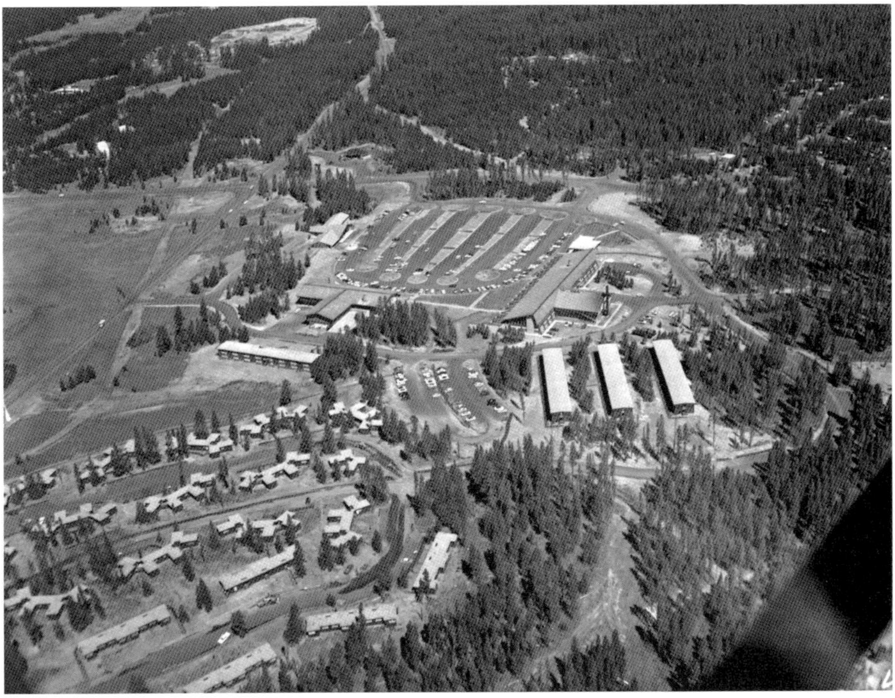

Construction at the large site was complicated by unclear division of labor between YPC and NPS, the short construction schedule and winter weather, August 1958. *Photo by Jack E. Boucher, courtesy of NPS, YNP, YELL 27102-1.*

cabin area, the water table was found to be near ground surface in all areas in the spring and did not seem to drop more than six feet." Matters were worsened when McNeil had to halt construction in fall 1956 (for weather), leaving thousands of feet of ditches dug and left open over winter. In the spring of 1957, it was faced with a "sea of mud."[154] YPC drained water from about fifty cabin sites and built temporary wooden walks "with the expectation that the NPS would soon commence landscaping."[155]

According to YPC, NPS stated that it didn't have the funds to rectify the water-soaked cabin site area, that YPC was forced to grade the site and plant vegetation to hold the soil—to make it presentable to the public. "It was to be a symbol of Mission 66, complete in every phase, for all the country to see; a fact that was as important for the Yellowstone Park Company as it was for the NPS."[156] This disagreement stemmed from differing interpretations of the new concession contract held between YPC and NPS.

Frost heaves were discovered by Yellowstone's landscape architect Frank Mattson in June 1959. He expressed no surprise at the results, as there were

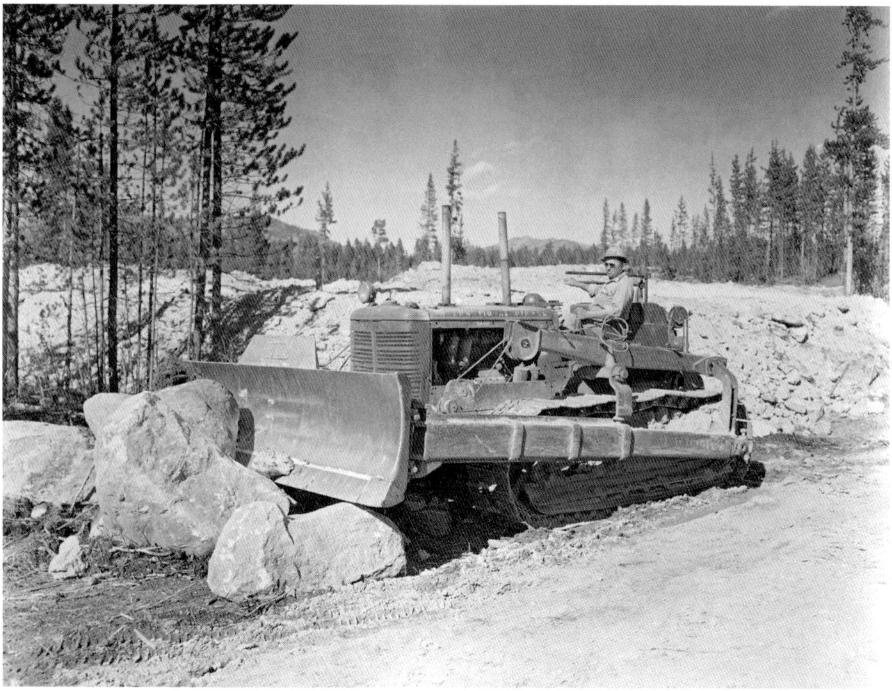

The site proved challenging to work with; rock and mud slowed progress, adding to the construction complications and errors discovered after completion. *YPC photo, courtesy NPS, YNP, YELL 185385-65.*

several wet spots in the area, which "could have been avoided, but there were some headstrong people involved and one was the Welton and Beckett Architect, Gilbert Lord. However, if the drilling which was done for the footings of the cabins had reasonable supervision, which was a responsibility of the architectural firm, we are quite sure there would be no trouble now. The holes were drilled some time before they were poured. In damp ground the sluffing would be a serious problem. They actually do not know just how deep the footings are because of lack of surveillance."[157]

The delay in the fall of 1956 had already caused the schedule to slip. The contract with McNeil provided for a completion date of July 1, 1957—provided that weather conditions at the job site permitted the contractor to work until December 1, 1956. On November 1, 1956, B.W. McNeil had written the following to Huntley Child Jr., vice-president of YPC:

> *Weather conditions at the site have now reached the state where it is impossible to continue the work on an efficient and economical basis.*

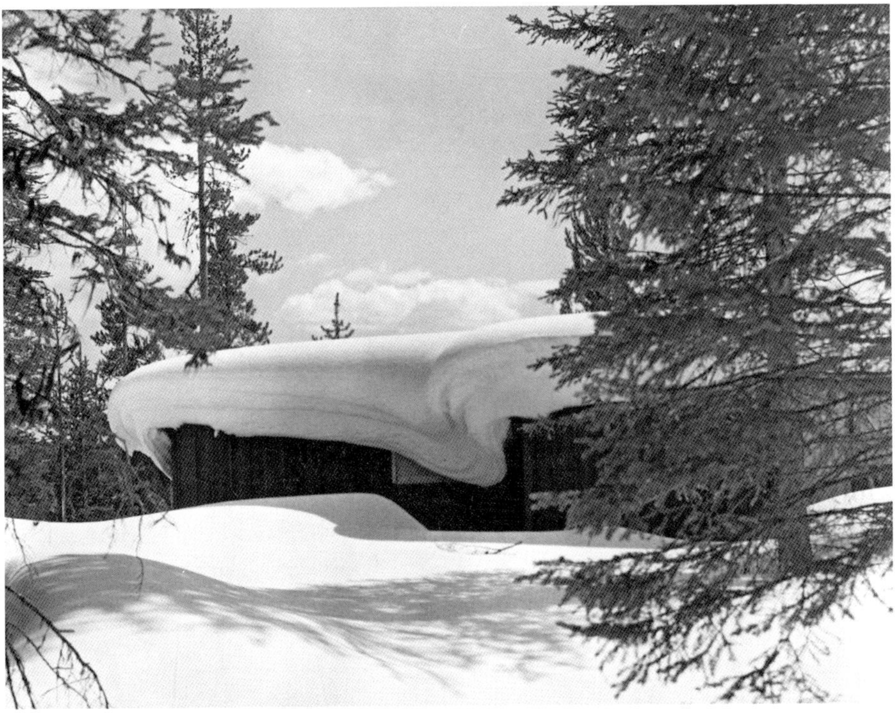

Snow and severe cold at the site delayed the start of construction in May 1956 and halted construction that fall. *YPC photo, courtesy NPS, YNP, YELL 185385-63.*

> *There is approximately 18 inches of snow on the ground and temperatures are ranging from below zero to a maximum of 30 degrees daily. We are advised that we cannot expect better conditions, on the contrary can expect further snow fall and lower temperatures. Will stop and winterize the project. Will need to change the completion date indicated in the contract. Since you're anxious to occupy by July 1, 1957, we won't close the construction camp down until November 17, 1956. Will close in the administration and lodge buildings and provide sufficient heat to provide satisfactory working conditions. Will resume operations on April 1, 1957. Then should have motels in A area substantially complete by July 1, 1957.*[158]

Although McNeil Construction was forced away from the job site, due to the severe winter, "A crew of men from McNeil worked during the winter in a steam-heated garage in Gardner, Mont. The walls and floors of the building were prefabricated in the garage, and in the spring were transported to the

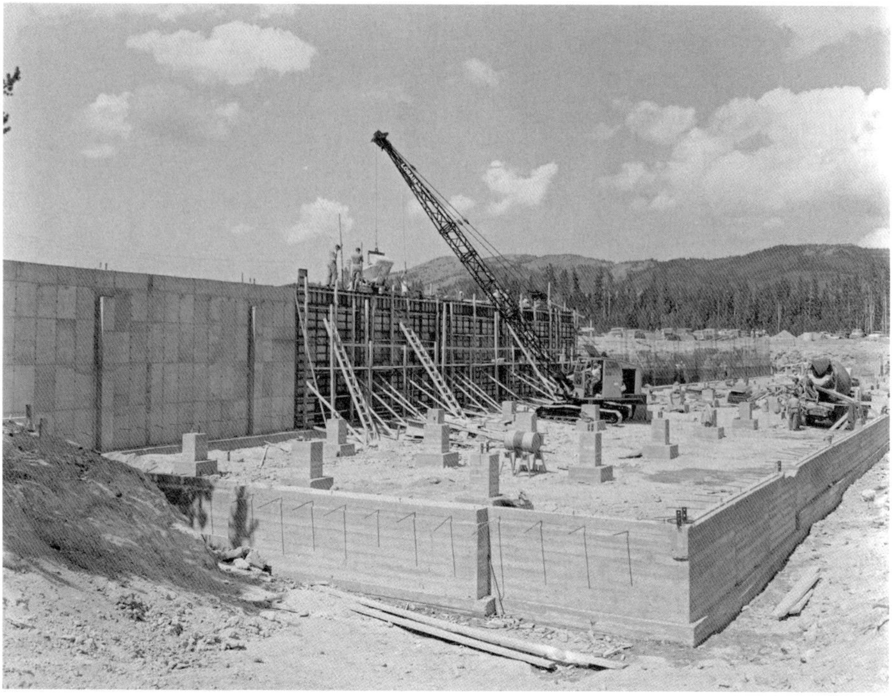

Canyon Village Lodge's large footprint required a large crew and large construction equipment, 1956. *YPC photo, courtesy NPS, YNP, YELL 185385-66.*

village, where they were lowered into position with a track-mounted crane. Roofs were added by carpenters at the village site."[159]

That the project was not substantially complete until August 1957 was not surprising, given the weather and site constraints, multiple changes to the scope of work and the complex coordination efforts required with the many personnel on site.

The Dedications

Construction of the lodge, Administration Building, dormitories and Hamilton Store was completed in August 1957, in time for the dedication on August 31. By this time, YPC had spent $5 million on the project and Hamilton and Haynes $3 million combined. Mr. and Mrs. Welton Becket attended, along with Welton M. Becket Jr., who recalled staying at Canyon

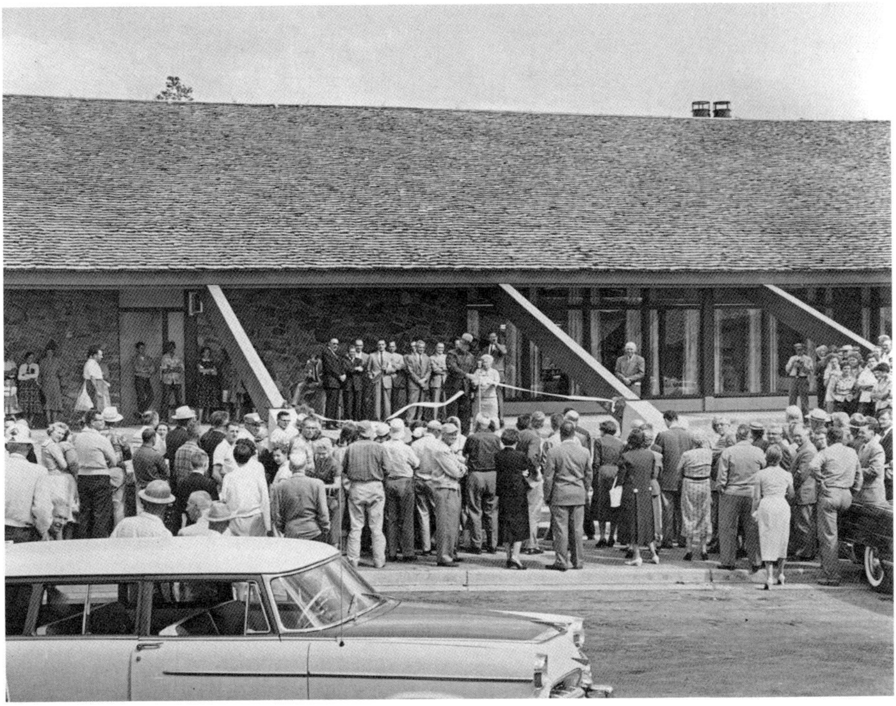

August 31, 1957 dedication ceremony at Canyon Village Lodge. *YPC photo, courtesy NPS, YNP, YELL 185385-64.*

Village just after it opened.[160] The *Salt Lake City Tribune* reported on June 23, 1957, that the "Charming, New Canyon Village" was opening July 1 and would be a "[c]omplete new village with all facilities near the incredible beauty of Grand Canyon. Massive lodge, 500 modern motel-type units with hot water, heat and showers."[161]

The Canyon Visitor Center was dedicated the next year, on August 17, 1958. NPS director Conrad Wirth, Secretary of the Interior Fred A. Seaton and Superintendent Lon Garrison were all present for the ribbon cutting ceremony. The dedication booklet glowed that "[f]rom it will radiate the visitor services offered by the Government, Information service, guided trips, interpretive talks, orientation programs, protection and evening campfire talks will original from here."[162]

Chapter 7
ACCEPTANCE OF CANYON VILLAGE

I know what I like.
—everyone

I Like What I Know (What They Really Mean)

Appreciation for architectural design is typically formed from a basis of understanding. The more a critic understands the design intent, how well a building provides for the needs impressed on it and how it responds to its site, the more the observer accepts the project. Those in architectural circles were always more in favor of Canyon Village and the other Mission 66 structures than laymen appeared to be. Public interpretation was mixed, primarily resulting from comparison with the picturesque buildings being replaced.

NPS director Wirth tried to manage public expectations through speaking engagements, television appearances and articles in various publications. Wirth reached out to the general public most successfully with the help of his supporter, the National Geographic Society. In a May 1958 issue of the society's magazine, he presented a black-and-white photograph of the exterior of Canyon Village Lodge and the Administration Building, citing "[t]he 'New Look' in Park Architecture: Yellowstone's Canyon Village Lodge," which he described as the "[f]irst development built during Mission 66, this new guest center lies within earshot of Yellowstone's thundering falls. Visitors stay in 500 motel-style units clustered beneath tall pines. The lodge, a split-level structure that stretches a city block, houses a dining room, cafeteria, lounge, photo studio, and gift shop."[163]

In the July 1966 issue of *National Geographic* magazine, Wirth expressed particular pride in the Canyon Village project, stating that it included the replacement of the old Canyon Lodge "perched near the rim of the Grand Canyon of the Yellowstone, the brown-stained shingle structure detracted from the site's natural beauty. Mission 66 permitted razing it and the old Canyon Hotel as well, and establishing a new Canyon Village Motor Lodge half a mile back from the canyon's rim. New trees on the old site restore the area as nearly as possible to the pristine beauty the park system is charged with preserving."[164] Wirth's public statements invariably referenced the resources being saved, reminding the public of the larger preservation issues that Mission 66 tackled.

Wirth also wrote frequently in the *National Parks Magazine*, a quarterly publication by the National Parks Association (an "independent, non-profit organization with nation-wide membership guarding America's heritage of scenic wilderness").[165] Journalists and readers used the magazine as a sounding board primarily to voice concern about the parks and what they viewed as the Park Service's apparent lack of concern for the preservation of the natural resources. Wirth's writings in this magazine helped to quell this anger by explaining the position and intents of the Park Service. In January–March 1958, he defended the new Canyon Village development by speaking to their fears and reaffirming that the "old Canyon lodge denied park visitors the most dramatic view of Upper Yellowstone Falls."[166] That he rarely spoke of the architectural design demonstrates his wisdom that the issue was larger than that.

Terminology was also deemed important. It had been decided by the Mission 66 Advisory Committee early on that it would be necessary to differentiate between the new lodge-and-cabin accommodations and the motels outside the national parks (as well as the earlier accommodations, which included a large hotel, lodge and cabins). The committee "recommended that the term 'motel' be discouraged as inappropriate for park use, and that the name 'lodge' be used, as more descriptive of the facilities and more appealing to the visiting public."[167]

YPC's new Canyon Village brochures spoke of "an enchanting new village with complete modern facilities set in the serene forest area near the incredible beauty of the Grand Canyon of the Yellowstone River."[168] Accompanied by colored rendered images of the cabins, the caption (black text on teal background) called them "cottage units." The lodge's list of amenities was complete and glamorous.

The Response

The opening of Canyon Village received considerable attention in the press around the country. The August 1957 travel section of the *Oakland Tribune* was prototypical in calling attention to the "New Look" at Yellowstone's Canyon development. The author described the "cottages" as of "modern, pre-fab design" and the lodge "of modern architecture, too." Noting that "at first it may be difficult for the visitor to reconcile modern design with the ageless surroundings of a mountain vacation retreat, where log cabins and rustic lodges are by tradition part of the landscape." He added that there were "compensations" in the interior, as though a consolation prize, for the designers had "utilized the natural colors of the park. The oranges and yellows from the rocky canyon of the nearby Yellowstone River are subtly blended with the blues and greens of the timbered mountainsides into lighting units, murals, upholstery and other décor." He influenced the reader by describing the site with "low, sweeping lines of the buildings tend to make the village less conspicuous than the old four-story lodges protruding to tree-top heights." He closed with the statement that the Park was still the same, little changed by the "New Look."[169]

The more vocal public reactions were negative, as is often the case. Montana's BLM supervisor informed NPS regional director Howard Baker, "It appears that at least some segments of the public are averse to the modernistic type of improvements that are being placed in the Park. No doubt this development has come to your attention."[170] The complaints were typically not about the architectural style but rather the type of improvements. Many felt that the parks were accruing too many resort-like features, yet the Park Service was actually removing those amenities—tow ropes for skiing and swimming pools, for example. Many felt that the parks should not have any overnight accommodations, yet Yellowstone was too large to do away with lodging in its interior. The argument over keeping the parks unimpaired and yet available was waged in the printed press regularly. Local businessmen in West Yellowstone described the situation as disastrous in their 1961 letter to Montana senator Lee Metcalf:

> *The gateway towns such as West Yellowstone depend entirely on tourist dollars for their very existence and most of the money is put right back in their business to expand and improve for the benefit of the tourists. We cannot see why our federal taxes are taken from us and then used against*

> *us to finance projects for concessionaires within the Parks. The people feel that it is unfair competition. These concessionaires pay no state or county taxes....If the tourists want to see Coney Island, then let them go to Coney Island. Lets* [sic] *don't make one out of the Parks.*[171]

Several journalists weighed in on the architectural aspects of the park developments. Devereux Butcher slammed modern architecture regularly in the *National Parks Magazine* and did not spare the Canyon Village project from his harsh words. Two snowed-on during-construction photographs of Canyon Lodge were treated to his following review: "The concession buildings in Yellowstone's new Canyon development are colossal in scale and of freak design." And "[t]o free the rims of the Canyon of the Yellowstone River of clutter is a most worthwhile project; but beyond that, we found little to praise....Man here is creating a 'feature' that will compete with the park's natural wonders for public attention. Conspicuous park structures violate the national policy governing our national parks."[172] Unfortunately, Butcher was not able to enter the lodge and experience the volume and views, although he would probably have objected to the vibrant colors. Readers did follow Butcher's lead, though, with one writing—regarding another victim of his pen—that "[i]t is comforting to know that you are watching such matters as the use of paint that almost screams in some of the national parks." Another "admired his crusade for better, less conspicuous designs of buildings in our national parks."[173]

The architectural community addressed this latter design problem, of creating a building that would blend with its surroundings and not be obtrusive. The rustic hotels of the early 1900s did not achieve this, with their towering scale and grandeur. In his January 1957 *Architectural Record* article about Mission 66, Emerson Goble shared his observation that the Park Service had been "schooled in the philosophy that 'any man-made structure is an intrusion on the scene.'"[174] Goble felt that "what this attitude has done to architectural design can be seen in one national park where a concessioner's hotel development turned out incredibly badly, largely because of this conviction that buildings are but necessary nuisances."[175] WB&A's rendering of the Canyon Village Lodge interior, which depicted the intended grace amid modern grandeur, was featured in the article. The space conveyed could almost have been anywhere. The connection to the exterior views, through nearly full-height glazing, is what fit it into the park. This is what could be classified as "not necessarily the most modest" objective offered by Goble.[176]

Perhaps the most reliable critique came from the Park Service itself, which organized an immediate analysis of the Canyon Village projects in September 1957. NPS personnel from across the country—park superintendents, regional directors and design chiefs—as well as architects and concessioners, attended the Park Development Conference convened at Grand Teton and Yellowstone National Parks in September 1957. Wirth's keynote address stated the conference objective to closely examine each park's Mission 66 improvements: "Whatever basic conclusion we may reach about each of the projects we shall see and study in Yellowstone and Grand Teton must be, in effect, an answer to the question, 'Is this directed toward the wisest and best use of this particular resource?' This is equally true of every element of the Mission 66 program."[177] Architect Eldridge T. Spencer (designer of Colter Bay Visitor Center and Yosemite Lodge) set the stage for architectural expectations with two pointed comments:

> *Architects designing in a National Park should design for use—for people—not design monuments for architects…* [and] *Overworked, decadent styles have no place in a National Park.*[178]

Ten teams reviewed the Mission 66 Canyon Village development and presented their findings on the final day of the conference. The teams admired the village concept and stated, "The general layout of the village area is excellently planned and carried out."[179] Team A's response to Canyon Lodge was representative: "We have nothing but praise for the main lodge building. The contemporary architectural treatment of the building was enthusiastically approved by all, though some sheepishly admitted they came here expecting to vote otherwise. Everything about the structure seemed to make the group happy." Team G favored the village area and wrote "that the architectural design established for the development is quite pleasing and appropriate, even though it is a radical change from structures in other park areas." Team I appears to have observed visitor reaction, providing the following useful comment about the lodge: "There is a demonstrated and excellent response to the facilities by visitors. The use of new colors and designs provide a most pleasing atmosphere."[180]

The remainder of the conference teams' comments were a variation on the theme of positive acceptance, with additional notes of recommended improvements for the cabins (soundproofing and luggage space), more restrooms for both the lodge and visitor center and other functional enhancements that were prophetic.

The Cabins

After the first season of renting the cabins, Yellowstone superintendent Lon Garrison was asked to share the cabin plans with his counterpart at Glacier National Park. He provided copies of the plans, along with the following comments regarding how they had been received:

> *Although you have not requested an opinion regarding these cabins, we believe it is only fair to say something about the reactions which people are expressing about their design and appearances, as well as what some of the other problems are in relation to the locations and building sites. The general reaction of most people or laymen has not been favorable. These cabins are entirely new installations in Yellowstone and, although they may have shortcomings from several points of view, they are a tremendous improvement over most of the overnight accommodations in the park. Each room will have a bath arrangement and heat and hot water will be provided. Economics have been a major factor in design and construction. The furnishings will go a long way toward improving their*

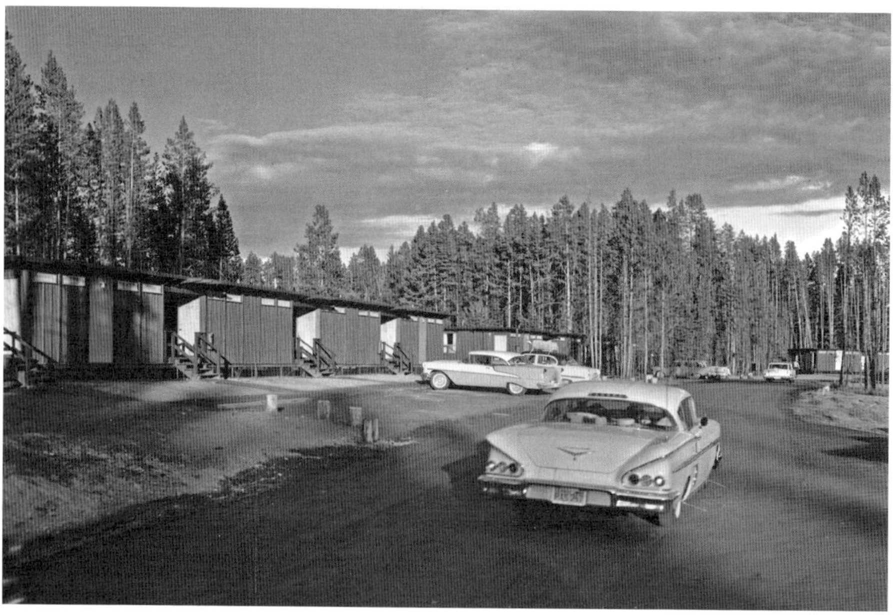

The Type A cabins looked like flat-roofed boxcars up on stilts, and the boards and battens were painted dark, August 8, 1958. *Photo by Jack E. Boucher, courtesy of NPS, YNP, YELL 29673-2.*

> *attractiveness....It is this completely flat roof which gives them the box car appearance.*[181]

The reaction to the cabins generally never improved, and the tides of taste changed over the years. The cabins' stature did not fare as well as the rest of the village's popularity.

Current Status

Canyon Village currently appears drab. Exterior wood has been painted Park Service brown, and the original colorful and playful signage has been replaced. The visitor center has been superseded with a larger, fine Arts & Crafts–style building that is out of place. The vibrancy of the interiors have been incrementally diminished, with painting over clear-finished wood, extensive carpeting, adjusting of interior volumes and removal of colors—in furniture, on light fixtures and from artwork.

Yellowstone National Park cultural resource staff have developed an appreciation for Mission 66 at Canyon Village—at least as a symbol of the origins of Mission 66 and perhaps for its sophisticated interiors. YNP entered into a Memorandum of Agreement with the Wyoming State

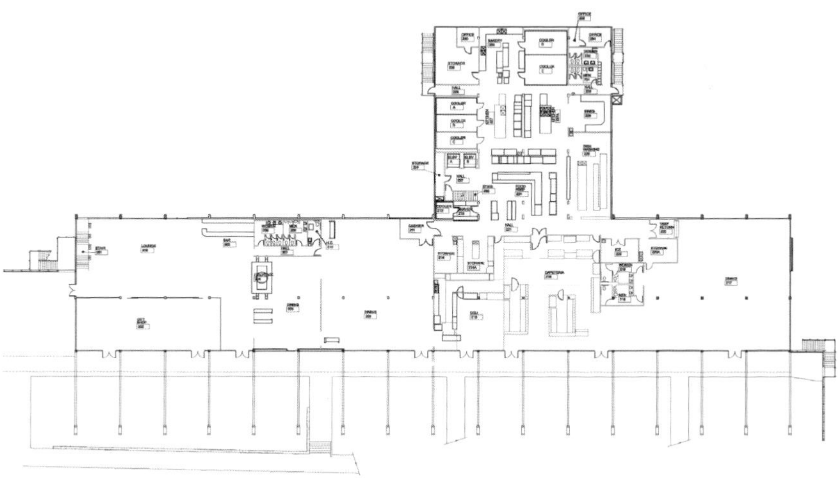

The 2015 floor plan of the main level of Canyon Village Lodge, depicting the current configuration. *Drawing by CTA Architects Engineers.*

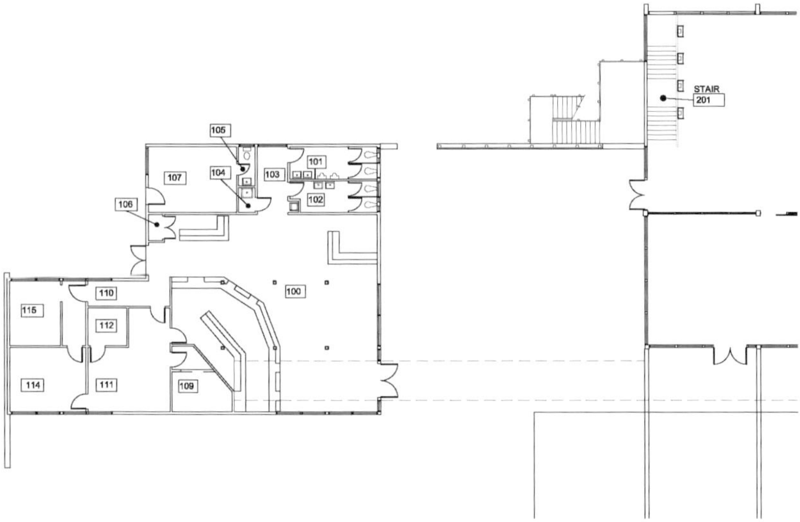

The 2015 floor plan of the Canyon Village Administration Building, depicting the current configuration. *Drawing by CTA Architects Engineers.*

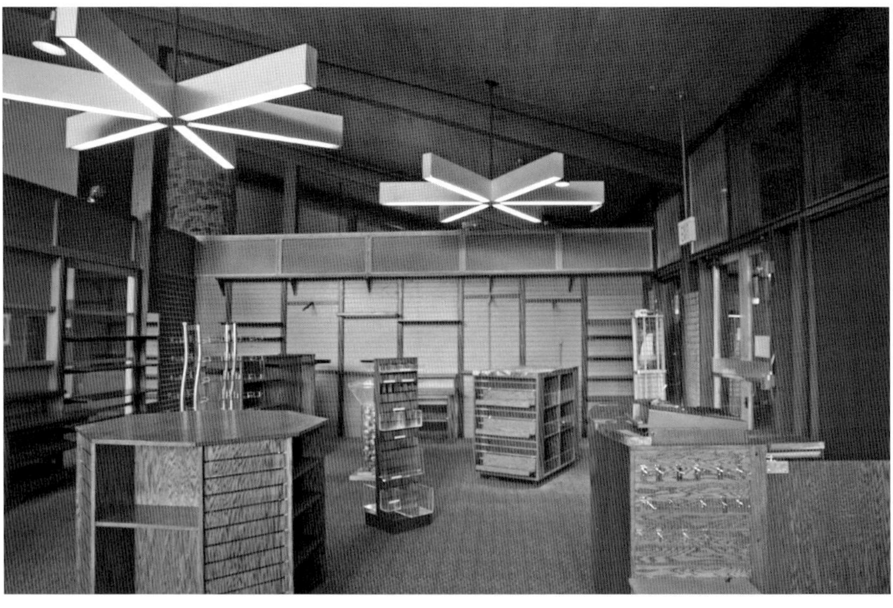

Canyon Village Lodge Gift Shop in 2015, looking south. *Photo by the author.*

Historic Preservation Office to study the history of the Canyon Village Lodge and Administration Building, in exchange (as mitigation for) the demolition of the cabins in Loops A and C. The study has informed the renovation of Canyon Lodge, as it is being transformed for new serving and dining experiences. The enhancement project, managed by the current concessioner Xanterra Parks & Resorts, will restore many of the original features of the lodge—the wood block flooring, the volumes, the colors, the back bar and the screen walls—and reintroduce modern-style furniture. Upon the lodge's reopening in May 2017, the visitor will recognize this Mission 66 resurrection and be able to judge it from a favorable distance of time. The Administration Building will be adapted for new uses after its functions (visitor overnight registration) have been relocated into one of the new lodges.

Chapter 8

THE FUTURE OF MISSION 66

Mission 66 and modern architecture is still a hard sell, especially to those who grew up with it. The aging of the buildings represents the viewer's personal aging. Perhaps that's why the younger generations have been able to embrace the modern era without the restraint of emotional baggage. The nation in general has been slow to embrace the architecture of the 1960s, not seeing the context of its response to function, economy, massively increased visitation, the prevalence of the automobile, material and construction advances and—in the Park's case—the protection of the natural resources. It is critical to not separate the architecture from these requirements and the grander goal of conservation.

Not every Mission 66 building was constructed of cheap materials—Canyon Village is an excellent example of good construction. Not every building is cold and uninviting. Like buildings of any style, some are better executed and some better received than others. Not all agree on what is the "best" example of the style.

Canyon Village was determined eligible for listing in the National Register of Historic Places in 2000. Canyon Village Lodge is considered a contributing resource within this potential historic district. It is hoped that NPS realizes the value of Canyon Village and that it will retain its solid place in the Mission 66 story. The "Recent Past" initiatives and the efforts of DOCOMOMO (International Committee for Documentation and Conservation of Buildings, Sites and Neighbourhoods of the Modern Movement) have helped to promote and protect significant works of the modern era.

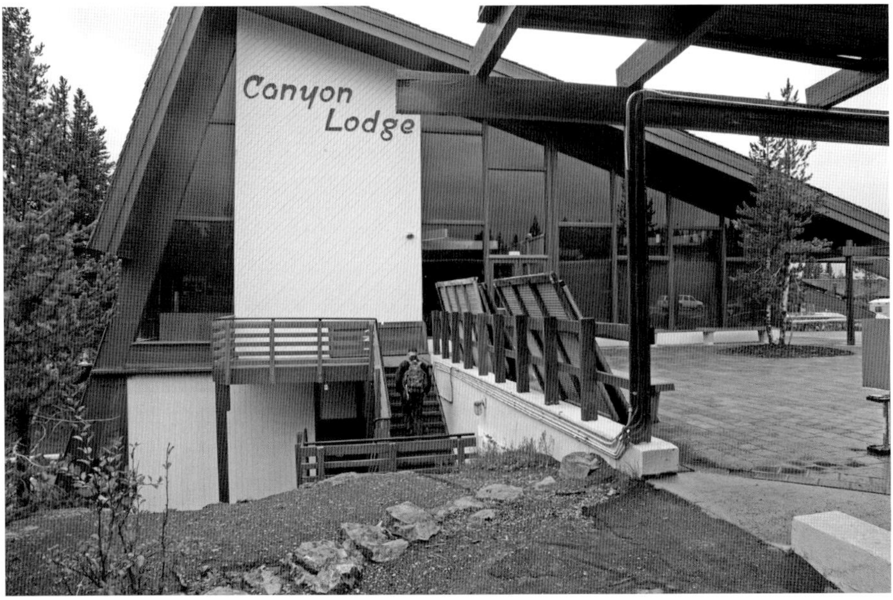

Terrace between Canyon Village Lodge and the Administration Building in 2015, looking south. *Photo by the author.*

The Park Service has responded unevenly to modern structures in the national parks. Richard Neutra's indisputable masterpiece, the Gettysburg Cyclorama, was demolished in 2013 after a fourteen-year debate regarding its appropriateness, use and worth. Two modern visitor centers in Glacier National Park—Logan Pass and St. Mary—have been well received, listed individually in the National Register of Historic Places and renovated. The case is typically larger than aesthetics and often reflects attitudes toward siting and park interpretation. An appreciation of the rich history of Mission 66 and the design objectives needs to be part of the conversation, or more of this past will be lost forever.

The renovation of Canyon Village Lodge bodes well for Yellowstone and will perhaps be a prototype for the rest of our national parks, as they celebrate the 100th anniversary of the National Park Service and the 50th anniversary of Mission 66.

NOTES

Chapter 1

1. Yellowstone National Park, "Mission 66 Prospectus," November 1955 (NPS-YNP, Coll. YELL 182385, Series 1, Box 21, Folder 1).
2. Newton B. Drury, NPS director, "Basic Philosophy of the National Park Service," in Haynes, *Haynes Guide*, 6.
3. YNP, "Annual Travel to Yellowstone and Annual Manhours of Uniformed Personnel," 1956 YNP Prospectus (NPS-YNP, Coll. YELL 182386 [2013 version], Series 1, Box 21, Folder 1).
4. Papineau, "Transforming Place at Canyon," 70.
5. Congressional Acts Pertaining to Yellowstone, "Military Assistance Authorized for Protecting the Park—Sundry Civil Bill for 1883," http://www.yellowstone-online.comhistory/yhfour.html.
6. Papineau, "Transforming Place at Canyon," 156.
7. Ibid., 182–201.

Chapter 2

8. Wirth, *Parks, Politics, and the People*, 234.
9. Ibid., 11.
10. Ibid., 14–18, quote from page 39.
11. Ibid.

12. Douglas Monday, letter to President Eisenhower, February 1, 1956 (NPS-YNP, Coll. YELL 185385 [2012 aid], Series 2-B, Box 9, Folder 2).
13. Howard W. Baker, Region II director, memo to superintendents, May 10, 1956 (NPS-YNP, Coll. YELL 182386 [2013 aid], Series 1, Box 20, Folder 10).
14. Conrad Wirth Informational Memorandum No. 2, to the Washington office and all field offices, March 17, 1955 (NPS-YNP Coll. YELL 182386, Series 1, Box 30, Folder 14: Mission 66: Correspondence + Memoranda, Instructional, 1955).
15. W.G. Carnes, Mission 66 staff chief, to NPS director Wirth, memorandum of Mission 66 Advisory Committee Meeting, May 14–17, 1956, 5 (NPS-YNP, YELL 182386, Series 1, Box 30, Folder 10: Mission 66: Advisory Committee, 1956).
16. W.G. Carnes, Mission 66 staff chief to NPS director Wirth, memorandum of Mission 66 Advisory Committee Meeting, May 14–17, 1956, 4 (NPS-YNP, YELL 182386, Series 1, Box 30, Folder 10: Mission 66: Advisory Committee, 1956).
17. Gilstrap, "Drive Planned to Save National Treasures," 4. Yellowstone's Haynes Photo Shop provided many of the images used in this series of articles.
18. Ibid., "Support of National Parks," 13.
19. Phillips Petroleum Company, *Your National Park System*, November 1964. NPS prepared the text.
20. Stewart Udall, press release, August 3, 1964 (NPS-YNP, Coll. YELL 185385 [2012 aid], Series 2-B, Box 13, Folder 2).
21. Conrad L. Wirth, approval of "Minutes from Meeting of Regional Directors and Chiefs, EODC and WODC, Washington Office, December 5–7, 1958," December 29, 1958 (NPS-YNP Coll. YELL 182386, Series 1, Box 31, Folder 5: Mission 66: Correspondence + Memoranda, 1958–59).

Chapter 3

22. Conrad L. Wirth, Informational Memorandum No. 1 (NPS-YNP Coll. YELL 182386, Series 1, Box 30, Folder 14: Mission 66: Correspondence + Memoranda, Instructional, 1955).
23. Conrad L. Wirth, Informational Memorandum No. 2, March 17, 1955 (NPS-YNP Coll. YELL 182386, Series 1, Box 30, Folder 14: Mission 66: Correspondence + Memoranda, Instructional, 1955).

24. Wirth, Informational Memorandum No. 2, March 17, 1955. Both Old Faithful Inn and Lodge were retained in their original locations.
25. Conrad L. Wirth, Informational Memorandum No. 3, June 27, 1955 (NPS-YNP Coll. YELL 182386, Series 1, Box 30, Folder 14: Mission 66: Correspondence + Memoranda, Instructional, 1955); National Park Service, "Mission 66 Report," September 1955, 46 (NPS-YNP YELL 182386, Series 1 Box 32, Folder 2: Mission 66: Development Programs 2/2).
26. Conrad L. Wirth, letter to William Nichols, May 9, 1955 (NPS-YNP Coll. 185385, Series 3, Box 76, Folder 2: Canyon Village, 1955–56); Wirth to Nichols, June 16, 1955 (NPS-YNP Coll. 182386, Series 1, Box 30, Folder 14: Mission 66: Correspondence + Memoranda, instructional 1955).
27. Wirth, *Parks, Politics, and the People*, 243.
28. Simpson, letter to Yellowstone superintendent Edmund Rogers, March 5, 1956 (NPS-YNP Coll. 182386 [2013 aid], Series 1, Box 20, Folder 10).
29. Mission 66 Advisory Committee meeting in D.C., memo to NPS director, May 18, 1956 (NPS-YNP Coll. YELL 182386 [2013 aid], Series 1, Box 8, Folder 11).
30. Yellowstone National Park, "Mission 66: Yellowstone National Park"; "Yellowstone National Park: Mission 66" (NPS-YNP Coll. 182386 [2013 aid], Series 1, Box 21, Folder 1).
31. William Nichols letter to Conrad Wirth, August 31, 1955 (MHS YPC collection 1-4).
32. Hugh Galusha Jr. to Tom Allen, September 15, 1955 (NPS-YNP Coll. YELL 185385, Series 8, Box 168, Folder 1: NPS, 1955).
33. Yellowstone Park Company Contract No. 14-10-0100-603 with National Park Service, executed February 3, 1956 (NPS-YNP, Coll. YELL 182386, Series 2-A, Box 6, Folder 7).
34. *Billings Gazette*, "Simpson Scores Concession Plan: Governor Declares More Funds Needed," September 22, 1955. As reported in Culpin, *History of Concession Development*, 147, this strategy might have been politically motivated. The Wyoming governor was a large stockholder in Husky Oil Company and was anxious to receive a contract to sell gasoline in the Park. Culpin cited Richard Bartlett, *Yellowstone: A Wilderness Besieged* (Tucson: University of Arizona Press, 1985), 369–80.
35. *Billings Gazette*, "Appraisal Firm Says Simpson's Concession Buying Plan Is Sound," September 9, 1955.
36. YPC Board of Directors' Annual Meeting Minutes, October 5, 1955 (MHS YPC Coll. Folder 1-4); Wyoming's consultant assessed YPC's

physical property in the Park at $4,912,000, with a reproduction cost of $15,787,238, *Billings Gazette*, September 9, 1955.

37. YPC, "Review of Contract Renewal and Building Program," August 31, 1956 (NPS-YNP Coll. YELL 185385 [2012 aid], Series 2-B, Box 9, Folder 2).

38. The Child and Nichols family concession fortunes have been amply and ably documented in several excellent publications. See Child, *Montana Pioneers*; Barringer, *Selling Yellowstone*; Haines, *Yellowstone Story*, vol. 2; Culpin, *History of Concession Development*; and others.

39. Barringer, *Selling Yellowstone*, 84–85.

40. Hugh Galusha Jr. to J.M. Potter, VO First National City Bank of New York, November 30, 1955 (NPS-YNP Coll. YELL 185385, Series 8, Box 168, Folder 1: NPS, 1955).

41. The sale of the Yellowstone Park Company and tale of subsequent owners has been provided by Culpin, *History of Concession Development*, 114.

42. Goss, *Serving the Faithful in Yellowstone*, 5–6.

43. Ibid., *Making Concessions in Yellowstone*; CTA Architects Engineers, *Lake General Store Historic Structure Report*.

44. Goss, *Making Concessions in Yellowstone*, 48–49; Culpin, *History of Concession Development*, 13, 25.

45. William Nichols, YPC, letter to Superintendent Edmund Rogers, June 15, 1956; and Charles Hamilton, letter to Superintendent Rogers, June 22, 1956 (NPS-YNP Coll. YELL 182386 [2013 aid], Series 1, Box 20, Folder 10). The underlined emphasis in Nichols's letter marks the only difference between his and Ham's letters.

46. Welton Becket & Associates, *WB: Vision…Through Supervision.*

47. Ibid.

48. Ibid., "Passing of a Great Man."

49. Ibid., *WB: Vision…Through Supervision.* Emphasis by the author, referencing specific items in Canyon Village Lodge and the cabins.

50. Ibid.

51. Hunt, *Total Design*, 4. The *WB Reporter*'s spring 1972 issue noted that at the time of publication, McGraw-Hill described the book as a "penetrating insight into the operations and inspirations of one of the nation's largest architectural and engineering firms." The author was a former editor of the *AIA Journal* and former senior editor of *Architectural Record*.

52. Architectural Resources Group, HABS CA-2860, "Furnace Creek Visitor Center, Death Valley National Park," 2010. Elaine Jackson-

Retondo, PhD, NPS, provided the history incorporated into the HABS documentation. This HABS report provides an excellent description of Cecil Doty's significant design contribution to a large number of national park visitor centers during the Mission 66 program.

53. Hunt, *Total Design*, 11, 16; *WB Reporter* (Spring 1969).

54. Becket, *Leadership in Architecture*, 69, 203.

55. AECOM has graciously authorized reproductions herein of WB&A's rendered images of Canyon Village.

56. The parenthetical job descriptions are provided by the October 1957 issue of the *WB Reporter*, which celebrated the formal opening ceremonies for the new $8 million Canyon Village. Welton Becket Jr. provided this newsletter to the author.

57. WB&A firm brochure, circa 1959, 3 (Getty Research Institute Special Collections, 2012.M.43 Becket Box 1, Folder 1).

58. WB&A firm brochure, 1954, and "Passing of a Great Man" (Getty Research Institute Special Collections, 2012.M.43 Becket Box 1, Folder 1, and Box 2, Folder 1).

59. *WB Reporter*, "Jack Beardwood Retires to Begin New Writing Career" (Fall 1972): 6 (Getty Research Institute Special Collections 2012.M.43, Box 2).

60. Letter from Jack B. Beardwood to Huntley Child Jr., January 2, 1956 (NPS-YNP Coll. YELL 185385 [2012 aid], Series 2-B, Box 9, Folder 2).

61. Frank Mattson memo to YNP superintendent, February 21, 1956 (NPS-YNP Coll. YELL 182386, Series 2, Box 9, Folder 1: Construction Projects, YPC, 1950–62).

62. *San Francisco Chronicle* obituaries for Ellis Kaplan (October 28, 2012) and Herb McLaughlin (July 7, 2015). MKD continues today as a multiethnic firm producing high-caliber design at an international level. Jim Diaz remains as a founding partner, serving as director of healthcare.

63. *Seminole Sentinel*, "Dallas to Get Ultra-Modern 28-Story Hotel," December 22, 1955.

64. Advertisement in *Los Angeles Times*, October 9, 1955, 29; *Los Angeles Times*, "Newly Completed," May 6, 1956, part 5, 11; *Los Angeles Times*, "Urban Revolt Going On, Architects' Parley Told: FHA Official Cites Los Angeles; Three Redevelopment Plans as Prime Example," May 17, 1956, 2.

65. Koyl, *AIA American Architects Directory*, 336, 713.

66. Wirth, *Parks, Politics, and the People*, 39.

67. It is believed that Hurt & Trudell prepared the final design documents for WODC, based on preliminary designs by NPS landscape architect Cecil Doty. Doty was the principal architectural designer of the WODC and provided many preliminary designs.
68. Bill Grabow, interview by the Bozeman Historic Preservation Advisory Board, March 11, 2010.
69. Thomas Allen, acting director, informational memo to Washington and all field offices, October 7, 1955 (NPS-YNP, Coll. YELL 182386, Series 1, Box 30, Folder 14: Mission 66: Correspondence + Memoranda, Instructional, 1955), 4.
70. Mattson, "Yellowstone." Frank Mattson's son, George Mattson, grew up in Mammoth, attended architecture school at Montana State College, worked on McNeil's construction crew at Canyon Village for two summers and now lives in Bozeman.
71. Carr, *Mission 66*, 141; Allaback, *Mission 66 Visitor Centers*, 248; Laura Soullière Harrison, "Painted Desert Inn National Register Nomination," 1986.
72. Dewey Livingstone, quoting CCC supervisor Harold Cole's personal recollections of completion of the interior finishes at the Painted Desert Inn, HABS AZ-161 written documentation of the Painted Desert Inn (1992), 25, 26.
73. Lon Garrison, letter to Mission 66 Advisory Committee chairman John Davis, August 13, 1957 (NPS-YNP, Coll. YELL 182386, Series 1, Box 30, Folder 10: Mission 66: Advisory Committee, 1956).

Chapter 4

74. Frank Mattson, Yellowstone National Park landscape architect, "Master Plan Development Outline Yellowstone National Park, Wyoming: Developed Areas—Canyon," November 1951 (NPS-YNP Coll. YELL 182386, Series 1, Box 20, Folder 2: Master Plan Development Outline, 1950–53).
75. Conrad Wirth, letter to William Nichols, YPC president, December 3, 1953 (NPS-YNP Coll. YELL 185385, Series 8, Box 168, Folder 1: National Park Service, 1955).
76. Smiley, *Pedestrian Modern*, 154–55.
77. WB&A's drawings include the dormitories in the "Commercial Area," yet since they are set outside of the raised portion dedicated to retail, this simpler interpretation is used throughout.

78. Grabow was the successor to his prior employer Fred Willson's firm. Willson had designed several buildings in the Park and had been involved in the Canyon Village planning efforts of the 1930s. Grabow designed the 1959 improvements to Haynes' Tower Photo Shop.
79. Thomas J. Hallin, director of construction engineering YPC, January 14, 1958 memo to YNP superintendent Garrison (NPS-YNP Coll. YELL 182386, Series 1, Box 31, Folder 5: Mission 66: Correspondence + Memoranda, 1958–59).
80. Goble, "Architecture (?) for the National Parks," 180.
81. Frank Mattson, letter to YNP superintendent, October 25, 1955 (NPS-YNP Coll. YELL 182386, Series 2, Box 6, Folder 11: Construction & Management, 1954–56).
82. Mattson to superintendent, October 25, 1955.
83. Mattson to superintendent, March 12, 1956 (NPS-YNP Coll. 182386 [2013 aid], Series 02-A, Box 3, Folder 2).
84. Frank Mattson, presentation at a park superintendents' conference, September 1957 (NPS-YNP Coll. YELL 182836 [2013 aid], Series 2-A, Box 5, Folder 11).
85. Frank Mattson, presentation at a park superintendent's conference, September 1957 (NPS-YNP Coll. YELL 182836 [2013 aid], Series 2-A, Box 5, Folder 11).
86. Bruce Becket, phone conversation with author, February 8, 2016.
87. WB&A drawing L-2, Job 1769, Main Lodge Building, January 24, 1957, "Bar Revisions" (Getty).
88. Orr Pickering & Associates, Canyon Village Lodge floor plans, July 31, 1959 (NPS-YNP Coll. YELL 185385, Series 3, Box 76, Folder 4: Canyon Village, 1960–63).
89. Special meeting of the YPC Board of Directors, minutes, August 16, 1958 (MHS Coll. NO. MC141, Folder 1-7).
90. Correspondence from March to April 1964 between Luis Gastellum, YNP acting superintendent, and George Beall (NPS-YNP Coll. YELL 185385 [2012 aid], Series 2-B, Box 13, Folder 1).
91. YPC, Review of Contract Renewal and Building Program—Canyon Village (NPS-YNP Coll. YELL 185385 [2012 aid], Series 2-B, Box 9, Folder 2).
92. June 24, 1956 press release (NPS-YNP Coll. YELL 185385 [2012 aid], Series 2-B, Box 9, Folder 2).
93. Frank Mattson to superintendent, October 25, 1955 (NPS-YNP Coll. YELL 182386 [2013 aid], Series 2-A, Box 6, Folder 7).

94. Undated drawing Sheet R-4 titled "Recreation Building Interior Elevations & Dets. Snack Bar & Stair Details" (Getty Research Institute Special Collections, Becket Collection 2010.M.83, Box 72). This is the only Recreation Hall drawing in the collection.
95. John S. Adams, landscape architect, YNP Developed Area Narrative, October 1968 (NPS-YNP Coll. YELL 182386 [2013 aid], Series 2, Box 18, Folder 4).
96. Superintendent Edmund B. Rogers, letter to Region II director, October 30, 1952 (NPS-YNP Coll. YELL 182386, Series 1, Box 11, Folder 3: Master Plans, 1951–53).
97. Letter from Jack Beardwood to Huntley Child Jr., January 2, 1956 (NPS-YNP Coll. YELL 185385 [2012 aid], Series 2-B, Box 9, Folder 2).
98. Frank Mattson, March 12, 1956 memo to YNP superintendent (NPS-YNP Coll. YELL 182386, Series 2, Box 9, Folder 1: Construction Projects, YPC, 1950–62).
99. Canyon Village Store Summary of Store and Dorm Construction Figures, undated (NPS-YNP Coll. YELL 182386, Series 2 Box 6, Folder 8: Construction Correspondence, 1956–57).
100. Ibid.
101. YNP superintendent submitted these to the region director on June 20, 1958, referencing drawing no. NP-YEL-8585-A (NPS-YNP Coll. YELL 182386 [2013 aid], Series 2-A, Box 5, Folder 11). A set of these drawings (no. 261), dated June 16, 1958, is in the Museum of the Rockies Special Collections (Povah Collection).
102. Team D park review, 1957 Park Development Conference, 61 (NPS-YNP Coll. YELL 185385, Series 8, Box 168, Folder 4: NPS, 1957).
103. Director Conrad Wirth, memo to all field office, February 10, 1956 (NPS-YNP Coll. YELL 182386 [2013 aid], Series 2-A, Box 8, Folder 5).
104. "Recommendations of the Mission 66 Advisory Committee," September 18–20, 1957, 4–5 (NPS-YNP Coll. YELL 182386, Series 1, Box 31, Folder 4: Mission 66: Correspondence & Memoranda, 1957–59).
105. Otto M. Brown, memo to acting superintendent, January 20, 1955 (NPS-YNP Coll. YELL 182386, Series 2, Box 6, Folder 11: Construction & Maintenance, 1954–56).
106. *Billings Gazette*, "Service Plans Park Projects: Agency Preparing for Construction," April 30, 1956 (NPS-YNP Coll. YELL 182386 [2013 aid], Series, Box 20, Folder 10).
107. This material was also used by Hurt & Trudell at the exterior of the Craters of the Moon Visitor Center in 1957. Given Cecil Doty's heavy

involvement in the design at Craters of the Moon, it's conceivable he influenced the design of the Canyon Visitor Center as well.

108. YNP superintendent Garrison, memo to WODC chief, October 11, 1957 (NPS-YNP Coll. YELL 182386 [2013 aid], Series 2-A, Box 8, Folder 4).

109. Report on the visitor center operation for 1959 season, November 19, 1959 (NPS-YNP Coll. YELL 182836, Series 2, Box 6, Folder 12: Construction Correspondence, 1959–61).

110. Kaeding, Chalfant, Young, Johnson and Madsen, "Environmental Assessment Canyon Visitor Center Rehabilitation."

111. Frank Mattson, memo to YNP superintendent, February 21, 1956, regarding January 23–February 10, 1956 trip to San Francisco (NPS-YNP Coll. YELL 182386, Series 2, Box 9, Folder 1: Construction Projects, YPC, 1950–62).

112. Mission 66: Prospectus (NPS-YNP Coll. YELL 182386, Series 1, Box 33, Folder 1: Mission 66: Prospectus).

113. Earlier estimates, in December 1955, of fabricating six cabins per day, and then erecting ten per day, proved unrealistic.

114. WB&A "Motel Cabins" plan sets dates April 9, 1956, and June 8, 1956, as used by McNeil during construction. These sets were loaned to the author by architect Herb Dawson of YNP, who bought them in a garage sale in the 1990s.

115. Mattson memo to YNP superintendent regarding trip to San Francisco, February 21, 1956 (NPS-YNP Coll. YELL 182386, Series 2, Box 9, Folder 1: Construction Projects YPC 1950–62).

116. Frank Mattson, memo to YNP superintendent, March 12, 1956, regarding Yellowstone conference with architects, builders and concessioner (NPS-YNP Coll. YELL 182386, Series 2, Box 9, Folder 1: Construction Projects, YPC, 1950–62).

117. *WB Reporter*, October 1957 (Getty Research Institute Special Collections, 2012.M.43 Becket 1).

118. YNP superintendent to Glacier superintendent, November 30, 1956 (NPS-YNP Coll. YELL 182386, Series 2, Box 6, Folder 8: Construction Correspondence, 1956–57).

119. Christopher Reynolds, "L.A.'s Invisible Builder: Long Overlooked, Welton Becket Is Getting His Due," *Los Angeles Times*, calendar tour of WB&A buildings, March 6, 2003, E39.

120. Lyle E. Bennett, WODC supervisory architect, to YNP superintendent, August 21, 1956 (NPS-YNP Coll. YELL 182386, Series 2, Box 6, Folder 8: Construction Correspondence, 1956–57).

121. Quotes from Welton Becket & Associates, *WB: Vision…Through Supervision.*
122. Bill Grabow, interview by the Bozeman Historic Preservation Advisory Board, March 11, 2010.
123. John M. Potter, letter to A.T. Hibbard, December 19, 1956; "Yellowstone Park Company Reconciliation of Funds Paid to Stone & Glass Ltd. 1957 Season" (NPS-YNP, Coll. YELL 185385, Series 8, Box 154, Folder 15: Stone & Glass Ltd., 1956–59).
124. Series of letters from February 20, 1958, through December 4, 1958 (NPS-YNP, Coll. YELL 185385, Series VIII, Box 154, Folder 15: Stone & Glass Ltd., 1956–59).

Chapter 5

125. Prudon, *Preservation of Modern Architecture*, 2.
126. Carr, *Mission 66*, 157.
127. Goble, "Architecture (?) for the National Parks," 178.
128. Eldridge T. Spencer, speech at the NPS 1957 Park Development Conference: Grand Teton and Yellowstone National Parks, September 10–17, 1957, 37 (NPS-YNP, Coll. YELL 185385, Series 8, Box 168, Folder 4: NPS, 1957).
129. Mission 66 Advisory Committee, "Q&A About Mission 66," typewritten carbon copy, January 1, 1956 (NPS-YNP, Coll. YELL 182386 [2013 aid], Series 1, Box 8, Folder 11).
130. *Billings Gazette*, "Canyon Village Construction Is First Park Expansion Job" (NPS-YNP, Coll. YELL 182386 [2013 aid], Series 2-A, Box 3, Folder 1).
131. The interior of the mezzanine was never built out due to budget cuts in June 1956. The large interior volume of the mezzanine became used for increasingly greater amounts of ductwork associated with the kitchen operations.
132. Bruce Becket, son of Welton Becket, in recalling the line art, opined that it was intended to pay homage to the American Indian. He stated that WB&A rarely consulted with interior designers outside its own firm, thus it was likely that it was designed by WB&A. Phone conversation with the author, February 8, 2016.

Chapter 6

133. Hal Broadhead, Yellowstone Park Service Stations manager, during interview by Zehra Osman, landscape architect, Yellowstone Center for Resources, as relayed to the author via e-mail, February 20, 2014.
134. R.H. Westlund, general superintendent for McNeil, letter to YNP superintendent Rogers, May 11, 1956 (NPS-YNP Coll. YELL 182386 [2013 aid], Series 2-A, Box, Folder 2).
135. Yellowstone Park Company summary, August 31, 1956 (NPS-YNP Coll. YELL 185385 [2012 aid], Series 2-B, Box 9, Folder 2).
136. Frank Mattson, presentation to park superintendent conference, September 1957 (NPS-YNP Coll. YELL 182386 [2013 aid], Series 2-A, Box 5, Folder 11).
137. Lemuel A. Garrison, YNP superintendent, to John Q. Nichols, November 6, 1958 (NPS-YNP, Coll. YELL 185385 [2012 aid], Series 2-B, Box 12, Folder 2).
138. Memo from Thomas J. Hallin, director of Construction and Engineering Department, to John Q. Nichols in La Jolla, December 4, 1958 (NPS-YNP Coll. YELL 185385 [2012 aid], Series 2-B, Box 12, Folder 2).
139. Ibid.
140. George Beall to YNP superintendent McLaughlin, August 27, 1964 (NPS-YNP Coll. YELL 185385 (2012 aid], Series 2-BN, Box 13, Folder 2).
141. All three quotes from "Outline of Ground Breaking," May 24, 1956 (NPS-YNP Coll. YELL 182386 (2013 aid], Series 2-A, Box 3, Folder 1).
142. Department of Interior press release, June 24, 1956 (NPS-YNP Coll. YELL 182386, Series 1, Box 30, Folder 15: Mission 66: Correspondence + Memoranda, Instructional, 1955–56).
143. The Canyon Hotel was not in the sacred proximity to the rim, yet it was built on unstable soils that drove up the cost of its necessary improvements.
144. Conrad L. Wirth, Groundbreaking Ceremony Address at Canyon Village, June 25, 1956 (NPS-YNP Coll. YELL 182386, Series 1, Box 30, Folder 15: Mission 66: Correspondence + Memoranda, Instructional, 1955–56).
145. Director Wirth, memo to Washington, D.C., office and all field offices, May 24, 1956 (NPS-YNP, Coll. YELL 182386, Series 1, Box 30, Folder 15: Mission 66: Correspondence + Memoranda, Instructional, 1955–56).
146. *Independent Record*, "Ground Breaking for Canyon Village Opens New Park Era," June 24, 1956, 1.

147. *The Canyon Village Special*, August 31, 1957 (NPS-YNP Coll. YELL 185385, Series 3, Box 76, Folder 2: Canyon Village, 1955–56).
148. McNeil Construction, "Job Cost Estimate, July 30, 1956" (NPS-YNP Coll. YELL 182386 [2013 aid], Series 2-A, Box 6, Folder 2).
149. Huntley Child Jr., letter to Lon Garrison, March 21, 1958 (NPS-YNP Coll. YELL 185385 [2012 aid], Series 2-B, Box 12, Folder 2).
150. DOI Press Release, September 26, 1956 (NPS-YNP Coll. 182386 YELL, Series 1, Box 30, Folder 15: Mission 66: Correspondence + Memoranda, instructional 1955–56).
151. DOI Press Release, October 6, 1956 (NPS-YNP, Coll. 182386 YELL, Series 1, Box 30, Folder 15: Mission 66: Correspondence + Memoranda, instructional 1955–56).
152. DOI Press Release, December 20, 1956 (NPS-YNP Coll. 182386 YELL, Series 1, Box 30, Folder 15: Mission 66: Correspondence + Memoranda, instructional 1955–56).
153. Canyon Environmental Assessment, 2001, National Park Service, 7.
154. Both quotes from Tom Hallin, YPC, to attorney Newel Gough, December 27, 1960 (NPS-YNP Coll. YELL 185385, Series 3, Box 76, Folder 3).
155. Tom Hallin, YPC, to attorney Newel Gough, December 27, 1960.
156. Ibid.
157. Frank Mattson, letter to assistant superintendent of YNP (NPS-YNP Coll. YELL 182386 [2013 aid], Series 2-A, Box 5, Folder 11).
158. McNeil, letter to Huntley Child Jr., November 1, 1956 (NPS-YNP Coll. YELL 185385, Series 3, Box 76, Folder 2: Canyon Village, 1955–56).
159. "Canyon Village Special," August 31, 1957 (NPS-YNP Coll, YELL 185385, Series 3, Box 76, Folder 2: Canyon Village, 1955–56).
160. Welton M. Becket Jr., e-mail to author, March 21, 2016.
161. *Salt Lake City Tribune*, June 23, 1957, 21. I am indebted to Kevin Koositra for showing me the electronic path to archival newspapers.
162. Canyon Visitor Center Dedication Booklet, August 17, 1958 (NPS-YNP Coll. YELL 185385, Series 3, Box 76, Folder 3).

Chapter 7

163. Wirth, "Heritage of Beauty and History," 616–17.
164. Ibid., "Today in Our National Parks," 27–30.
165. *National Parks Magazine* (January–March 1958).

166. Wirth, "Mission 66 in the Headlines," 9, 36.
167. Mission 66 Advisory Committee memo to NPS director, May 18, 1956 (NPS-YNP Coll. YELL 182386 [2013 aid], Series 1, Box 8, Folder 11).
168. Canyon Village brochure (NPS-YNP Coll. YELL 185385, Series 3, Box 76, Folder 4).
169. All quotes in this paragraph from Cathro, "'New Look' at Yellowstone Park."
170. R.D. Nielson, state supervisor of BLM, letter to Howard Baker, June 15, 1958 (NPS-YNP Coll. YELL 182386, Series 1, Box 31, Folder 5: Mission 66: Correspondence + Memoranda, 1958–59).
171. West Yellowstone Montana Chamber of Commerce, February 14, 1961 letter to Senator Lee Metcalf (NPS-YNP, Coll. YELL 182386, Series 1, Box 31, Folder 6: Mission 66: Correspondence + Memoranda, 1960–62).
172. Butcher, "Sunshine and Blizzard," 28–29.
173. Letters, *National Parks Magazine* (April–June 1957): 91.
174. Goble, "Architecture (?) for the National Parks," 178.
175. Ibid., 178.
176. Ibid., 174.
177. Conrad L. Wirth, introductory words at the 1957 Park Development Conference, September 10, 1957 (NPS-YNP Coll. YELL 185385, Series 8, Box 168, Folder 4: NPS, 1957).
178. Eldridge T. Spencer, speech at the 1957 Park Development Conference, September 10, 1957, 35–37 (NPS-YNP Coll. YELL 185385, Series 8, Box 168, Folder 4: NPS, 1957).
179. Team E, comments during the 1957 Park Development Conference (NPS-YNP Coll. YELL 185385, Series 8, Box 168, Folder 4: NPS, 1957).
180. Team comments during the 1957 Park Development Conference (NPS-YNP Coll. YELL 185385, Series 8, Box 168, Folder 4: NPS, 1957).
181. Lon Garrison letter to Glacier superintendent, November 30, 1956 (NPS-YNP Coll. YELL 182386 [2013 aid], Series 2-A, Box 4, Folder 9).

BIBLIOGRAPHY

Allaback, Sarah. *Mission 66 Visitor Centers: The History of a Building Type*. Washington, D.C.: National Park Service, Department of the Interior, 2000.

Barringer, Mark Daniel. *Selling Yellowstone: Capitalism and the Construction of Nature*. Lawrence: University Press of Kansas, 2002.

Becket, MacDonald, FAIA. *Leadership in Architecture: My Passion in Life*. Bloomington, IN: AuthorHouse, 2014.

Butcher, Devereux. "Sunshine and Blizzard: Afield with Your Representative." *National Parks Magazine* (January–March 1956). National Parks Association, Washington, D.C.

Carr, Ethan. *Mission 66: Modernism and the National Park Dilemma*. Amherst: University of Massachusetts Press, 2007.

Cathro, Morton. "The 'New Look' at Yellowstone Park." *Oakland Tribune*, August 25, 1957, C-3.

Child, Harry W., II. *Montana Pioneers: The Huntley, Child & Dean Families*. N.p.: self-published, 2009.

CTA Architects Engineers. *Lake General Store Historic Structure Report*, 2009. National Park Service.

Culpin, Mary Shivers. *A History of Concession Development in Yellowstone National Park: 1872–1966*. Wyoming: National Park Service, Yellowstone Center for Resources, 2003.

Gilstrap, Max K. "Drive Planned to Save National Treasures: National Park 'Mission' Set to Provide Better Service." *Christian Science Monitor*, September 22, 1955.

———. "Support of National Parks: A Public Responsibility." *Christian Science Monitor*, May 3, 1956.

Goble, Emerson. "Architecture (?) for the National Parks: Mission 66 Program Promises 10 Years of Opportunities and Arguments in the World's Most Wonderful Sites." *Architectural Record* (January 1957).

Goss, Robert V. *Making Concessions in Yellowstone*. 4th ed. N.p.: self-published, 2004.

———. *Serving the Faithful in Yellowstone: Henry Klamer and the General Store in the Upper Geyser Basin*. N.p.: self-published, 2003.

Haines, Aubrey L. *The Yellowstone Story: A History of Our First National Park*. Rev. ed. Vol. 2. Boulder: University Press of Colorado, 1997.

Haynes, Jack Ellis. *Haynes Guide: Yellowstone National Park*. N.p.: Haynes Inc., 1948.

Hunt, William Dudley, Jr., FAIA. *Total Design: Architecture of Welton Becket and Associates*. New York: McGraw-Hill Book Company, 1972.

Kaeding, Beth, Diane Chalfant, Linda Young, Lon Johnson and Doug Madsen. "Environmental Assessment Canyon Visitor Center Rehabilitation." February 2001. https://www.nps.gov/yell/learn/management/upload/ceapub.pdf.

Koyl, George S., ed. *AIA American Architects Directory*. American Institute of Architects. New York: R.R. Bowker, 1962.

Mattson, George. "Yellowstone: A Personal History." Presented to the Bozeman Quest for Knowledge Club, September 17, 2002.

Oakland Tribune. August 25, 1957.

Papineau, Diane Marie. "Transforming Place at Canyon: Politics and Settlement Creation in Yellowstone National Park." Master's thesis, Montana State University, April 2008.

Phillips Petroleum Company. *Your National Park System: A Passport to Adventure*. November 1964.

Prudon, Theodore H.M. *Preservation of Modern Architecture*. Hoboken, NJ: John Wiley & Sons Inc., 2008.

Smiley, David. *Pedestrian Modern: Shopping and American Architecture, 1925–1956*. Minneapolis: University of Minnesota Press, 2013.

Welton Becket & Associates. "The Passing of a Great Man." *WB Reporter* (Spring 1969). Getty Research Institute, Special Collections 2012.M.43 Becket 1.

———. *WB: Vision…Through Supervision*. Firm brochure, circa 1954. Getty Research Institute, Special Collections 2012.M.43 Becket 1.

Wirth, Conrad L. "Heritage of Beauty and History: Want a Live Volcano? Dinosaur Bones? Buffaloes? Sequoia Forest? Americans Own These and Much More—in the National Parks." In *Parks & Scenery: Heritage of Beauty and History*. Angwin, CA: Angwin Book Bindery. Article previously published in *National Geographic Magazine* 113, no. 5 (May 1958).

———. "Mission 66 in the Headlines." *National Parks Magazine* (January–March 1958).

———. *Parks, Politics, and the People*. Norman: University of Oklahoma, 1980.

———. "Today in Our National Parks: The Mission Called 66." *National Geographic* (July 1966): 27–30. Washington D.C.: National Geographic Society.

INDEX

A

Albright, Horace 20

B

Baker, Howard 23, 29, 109
Beardwood, Jack 42, 43, 64
Becket, Bruce 8
Becket, MacDonald 42
Becket, Welton D. 40, 41, 42, 43, 75, 76, 104
Bennett, Lyle E. 39, 46, 47, 75
Butcher, Devereux 110

C

cabins 30, 33, 40, 43, 50, 52, 53, 56, 61, 64, 72, 73, 74, 75, 76, 77, 81, 87, 89, 91, 92, 94, 95, 100, 101, 102, 108, 109, 112, 113, 115
Campbell, Jack 42
Canyon Hotel 16, 18, 34, 63, 70, 97, 108
Canyon Village Administration Building 33, 35, 52, 56, 60, 62, 67, 70, 82, 86, 87, 94, 100, 104, 107, 115
Canyon Village Lodge 18, 28, 33, 35, 52, 53, 56, 57, 62, 63, 64, 65, 70, 76, 77, 82, 84, 86, 87, 89, 90, 91, 94, 96, 97, 100, 104, 107, 108, 109, 110, 111, 112, 115, 117, 118
Canyon Village Recreation Hall 30, 33, 50, 60, 62, 63, 72, 82
Canyon Village Visitor Center 30, 44, 45, 46, 52, 66, 67, 68, 69, 70, 105, 112, 113
Child, Harry 16, 34, 35
Child, Huntley, Jr. 34, 35, 77, 102
Civilian Conservation Corps (CCC) 19, 20, 47

Cole, Tom 42
colors 36, 41, 47, 52, 53, 55, 68, 75, 87, 89, 90, 109, 110, 111, 115
CTA Architects Engineers 7, 69

D

dedication ceremonies 25, 38, 44, 68, 104, 105
D'Ewart, Wesley A. 97
dormitories 30, 33, 43, 52, 60, 61, 63, 64, 70, 72, 76, 77, 87, 100, 104
Doty, Cecil 42, 44

E

Eastern Office of Design & Construction (EODC) 21, 81
Eisenhower, President Dwight D. 21, 22, 43

F

Furnace Creek Visitor Center 42, 44

G

Galusha, Hugh D., Jr. 34
Garrison, Lemuel (Lon) 21, 48, 58, 68, 94, 105, 112
Gilstrap, Max 24
Goble, Emerson 110
Grabow, William "Bill" 37, 45, 52, 65, 77
Grand Canyon of the Yellowstone 14, 15, 49, 108
groundbreaking ceremonies 38, 43, 60, 63, 76, 96, 97, 98

H

Hallin, Thomas J. 94
Hamilton, Charles A. 35, 36, 38, 43, 98
Hamilton Stores 30, 31, 32, 33, 35, 36, 37, 38, 39, 42, 97, 99
Haynes, Frank J. 37
Haynes, Jack Ellis 37, 38
Haynes Photo (Picture) Shop 18, 33, 36, 37, 38, 45, 52, 65, 66
Hunt, William Dudley, Jr. 41
Hurt & Trudell 44, 52, 67

K

Kaplan, Ellis 42, 43, 44

L

line art 56, 57, 60, 89
Lord, Gilbert 42, 43, 55, 99, 102

M

materials (construction) 36, 47, 52, 56, 64, 65, 75, 76, 79, 80, 81, 87, 88, 89, 99, 117
Mather, Steven 20, 28
Mattson, Frank 39, 44, 46, 48, 49, 54, 55, 56, 62, 64, 72, 74, 94, 101
McNeil, Bruce 99
McNeil Construction Company (MCC) 50, 55, 72, 99, 103

Mission 66 Advisory Committee 21, 23, 30, 67, 108
Mission 66 prospectus 72
Mission 66 Steering Committee 21, 27, 28, 29
Mount Rainier National Park 28

N

Nichols, John Q. 34, 35, 38, 94
Nichols, William "Billie" 34, 35, 38

P

parking lot, horseshoe-shaped 11, 51, 87
Perkins, Dick 42
Plummer, Charles F. 41
Povah, Trevor 33, 36, 38

R

Rogers, Edmund B. 29, 38, 97, 99

S

"sacred zone" 16, 49
Seaton, Fred A. 105
Simpson, Milward L. 32
site development challenges 100
Spencer, Eldridge T. 81, 111
Stone & Glass Ltd. (S&G) 77, 94

V

Vint, Thomas 50

W

Western Office of Design & Construction (WODC) 21, 39, 42, 43, 46, 48, 68, 75, 81
Wirth, Conrad 11, 19, 20, 21, 23, 24, 27, 28, 29, 30, 31, 32, 45, 50, 67, 79, 81, 96, 97, 98, 105, 107, 108, 111
Wurdeman, Walter 40, 41

X

Xanterra Parks & Resorts 35, 115

Y

Yellowstone National Park 13, 21, 29, 37, 38, 39, 43, 45, 46, 48, 49, 62, 64, 67, 68, 70, 72, 75, 95, 97, 98, 111, 115
Yellowstone Park Company (YPC) 16, 28, 29, 30, 31, 32, 33, 34, 35, 38, 39, 40, 42, 50, 52, 53, 56, 58, 59, 60, 63, 64, 70, 72, 75, 77, 91, 94, 95, 96, 97, 98, 99, 100, 101, 102, 104, 108
Yosemite National Park 14

ABOUT THE AUTHOR

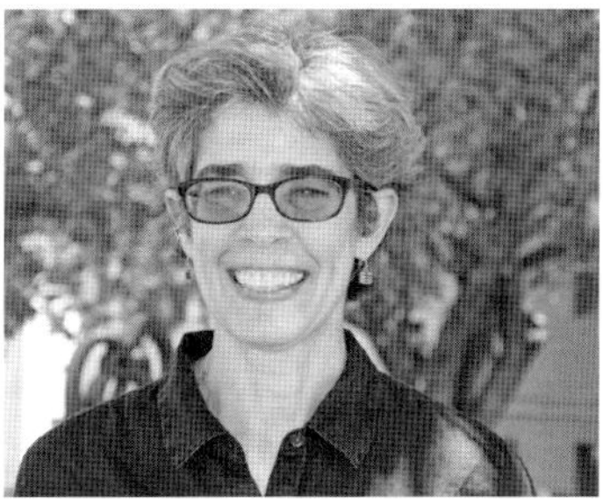

Lesley M. Gilmore is a licensed architect who has been director of CTA's Historic Preservation Services since 2006. In that capacity, she has worked on the preservation of historic properties in Yellowstone National Park and other national parks across the country. She became more immersed in the study of modern architecture when engaged by the General Services Administration to evaluate several of its modern federal courthouses. Her recent work on the renovation of Canyon Village Lodge has given her the opportunity to delve deeply into the lives of those working for the National Park Service, the Yellowstone Park Company and the architecture firm of Welton Becket & Associates when this seminal Mission 66 project was planned in 1955. Lesley and her husband, Bob Franzen, live in Gallatin Gateway, Montana, a one-and-a-half-hour drive from Yellowstone National Park.